Hey Doc

Its okay to carry

more than a driver &

Putter in your bag!

My Best

R. Hoagwood

MMXI

Mike

PRIMROSE U.S.M.C.

First Tour - Rescue

by

R. Michael Haigwood

authorHOUSE®

AuthorHouse™
1663 Liberty Drive, Suite 200
Bloomington, IN 47403
www.authorhouse.com
Phone: 1-800-839-8640

First published by AuthorHouse 11/3/2008

ISBN: 978-1-4389-0136-7 (sc)
ISBN: 978-1-4389-2304-8 (hc)

Library of Congress Control Number: 2008910284

Printed in the United States of America
Bloomington, Indiana

This book is printed on acid-free paper.

Thanks to those who gave inspiration for the characters:

Robert J. Nakonieczny, USMC
Michael J. Nakonieczny, USMC
Thomas P. (Maddog) Naughton, USMC
H. C. Bowden, USMC
T. J. Martinez, .USMC
Two Case Chapman, USMC
Harold Davidson, USN
Larry Hauder , USN
Mac McKenzie, USN
Gary Kruegar, USN
W. D. (Butch) Schroder, USA
R. P. Sullivan, USA
John La Mont, USA.
Ronni Sullivan, Civilian
Jerry McElligott, Civilian
Gus (Sweet Freddie) Fuson, American Indian

"I am convinced that there is no smarter, handier, or more adaptable body of troops in the world."

Winston Churchill, on the United States Marine Corps

CHAPTER 1

Las Vegas, Nevada

I walked into the Marine/Navy recruiting office two blocks off Fremont Street in Las Vegas, Nevada, on a very hot August day in 1966 to re-enlist in the Corps. A very large first sergeant greeted me with a vice-grip handshake and a wide smile. By the look in his eyes, he might be close to filling his quota for the month. When I announced my intentions to re-enlist, his smile faded a little, and I guessed re-ups didn't count.

The first sergeant released my crushed hand and said, "My name is First Sergeant Kelly. And who might you be, young man?"

"My name is Zachary Taylor Primrose, former corporal, United States Marine Corps."

"When were you released, Corporal Primrose?"

"My four-year tour ended on 1 January 1965, at the Marine Corps Supply Center, Yermo, California."

"Well, Corporal Primrose, I think you're off your rocker. You've served your country, what's the hurry to go get yourself killed?"

The recruiting office was old and worn, like First Sergeant Kelly, a WWII veteran and close to retirement. A two-story building left over

1

from the thirties housed the office, and the first floor had a porch that extended across the front, where in years past, people would sit out in their rocking chairs and suspended swings to enjoy the night air.

Inside, the office was cool and noisy with the swamp cooler going full blast: every paper not weighted down sailed across the small desk area.

First Sergeant Kelly's desk was on the port side as you walked in the door and the Navy recruiter was on the starboard, with the Marine captain's desk just through the door to the former kitchen area.

Five years ago I had walked through the same door to enlist and see the world. My intentions were to go by ship for the tour, but the Navy recruiter was out to lunch, and I was ambushed by a Marine sergeant. Before I could blink, the test was in front of me, and—not far behind—my signature was on the dotted line. The next thing I knew, the Greyhound bus depot speaker was screaming, "ALL ABOARD for Los Angeles, Long Beach, and points south." The YMCA in Long Beach was next, for a final physical, then the last leg to Marine Corps Recruit Depot, San Diego, California. The events seemed like a hundred years ago, instead of five.

I shook the past out of my head to focus on Sergeant Kelly telling me about re-enlistment bonuses. When he finished, I told him all I wanted was a guarantee for recon and assignment to Vietnam. "I'll bring your request up with the captain when he returns. Stop by later today, and in the meantime I'll make some calls about your service record book."

#

"Did I hear you right, Top? Did you say this former corporal wants to re-enlist with guarantees? We don't make pledges. He should know that."

"Yes sir, he wants recon training and assignment directly to Vietnam instead of a re-enlistment bonus."

"Okay, Top, this guy has already served his four years, right? Why does he want to go in harm's way when he doesn't have to?"

"Sir, when he was in MCRD, he made a big mistake when the drill instructor asked whether anyone could type. Primrose said he could, and that was the beginning of his tour as an office pough. He had originally put in for Combat Engineers and thinks he was mistrained and misassigned. He would like to be where the action is and make up for lost time."

"Top, send Primrose in when he returns. Where do these guys come from that are willing to go to all the hot spots in the world? Is it adventure they seek, or are they running from something? What's your take on Primrose?"

"Sir, I think Primrose is running from or looking for something he can't find in civilian life, but he appears to be a good man."

"Okay, send him right in when he returns."

"Yes sir."

#

When I returned to the recruiting office, First Sergeant Kelly said the captain was in and would entertain my aspirations for another tour.

I knocked on the doorjamb; the captain looked up and motioned me to enter. Marching in, I halted one foot from his desk, a habit retained from boot camp.

Captain Erndt looked me straight in the eye and wanted to know why he should allow me another four years in his Marine Corps.

"Sir, because the Corps was the best thing that ever happened to me, and I'd like to give something back and serve my country again, only this time in a more challenging assignment."

3

The captain nodded and then asked if there was anything in my civilian life he needed to know about that might disqualify me from re-enlistment! I replied that, having been out only a year, there was nothing to hide.

"Primrose, report out to First Sergeant Kelly. If he wants to re-enlist you, I'll support your request, but we can't guarantee anything. We can get you to recon training at Camp Pendleton, but if you fail that, it's Nam and office pinky for you."

"No need to worry about that; I won't fail recon, sir."

Top Kelly had the required papers typed up and in order for my signature. The physical would be next, followed by the records check, and—if all went well—I'd be on my way. With the papers signed, I thanked Top Kelly and headed back out to the street. I'd miss the swamp cooler blowing cold air throughout the recruiting office—outside was a scorcher.

Walking back towards Fremont Street in what the locals call a dry heat, I was thinking my number one priority was getting to Nam as soon as possible. If the re-enlistment somehow got sidetracked, I'd try for the Navy Seal Program or the Brown Water Navy. Having finished a tour of duty, I knew how the system worked; sometimes something very simple could bring the whole process to a screeching halt. "Just sign me up and ship me out." How complicated could that be?

#

According to the sketchy reports from the Department of Defense, the missing trio of musicians from a USO tour had not been heard from. The limited information coming through channels indicated the trio had been taken from a convoy up near the border with Laos and a ransom note was expected.

The Feds had informed me of the kidnapping, but they were vague, and I wondered if they had given me the whole story. According to their version, the trio and their bodyguards were heading for an engagement when the convoy was ambushed on the main road. The guards were killed and the trucks destroyed. So far there had been no demand for ransom to sell the trio back to friendly hands. The Feds proposed another scenario that might come into play, which would have the bad guys use the trio for their own pleasure and, when they tired of them, kill the two men and sell the woman. There were other scenarios, too ugly to even think about.

The government men said they would let me know if any more information came their way. The skinny one of the duo said, "You know if the trio had been with a larger and official USO tour group, they would've had better protection."

The skinny guy's fat partner was cold and heartless and suggested I keep my nose out of things, that they would handle the situation, but I got the impression that they had already written the trio off. With a war going on, the trio's disappearance was not on anyone's priority list. Their last words were "We'll keep in touch."

I knew they didn't give a rat's ass about the kidnapping, but to me it was personal—the trio included my wife, her father, and a family friend. They were family, and I had no choice but to take matters into my own hands. The journey to the hostile environment of Vietnam was about to start in earnest.

Rhonda and I had been married less than a year when the opportunity came up for her to take a six-month tour of the Far East, with her dad Fred and his friend Jack Mont—The Jack Mont Trio.

Fred and Jack had had a pleasant and uneventful tour the year before, and I based my decision to let her join the group on the merits of the last tour. The fact she would be with her father made the choice a little easier, and the point that both Fred and Jack were WWII veterans helped ease the worry for her safety.

The tour would've helped her career as a singer, bass player, and comedian. Six months on stage in front of thousands of service men and women was the best experience she could get, and getting paid for doing what she loved while touring the Far East surely was a plus. Getting captured by the enemy was not in the game plan.

I was finding the process of getting overseas to be agonizingly slow. The last communication with Rhonda had been from the Island of Guam, where they were playing at the Officer's Club and the Navy Enlisted Club. My brother-in-law, Mac McKenzie, was stationed there with the Naval Medical Facility. Mac had been a corpsman for the Marine Corps in Korea and Vietnam. I might could use his talent down the road.

Looking back, I should not have let her go, but hindsight is twenty-twenty. My hopes and prayers were that things got moving before bad things happened. If bad things happened I wanted to be in a position for some payback; the revenge would be sweet.

#

When Wednesday rolled around, I returned to the recruiting office to check in with Top Kelly, but there was a gunnery sergeant sitting at the Marine desk.

I pulled up to the desk and asked, "Where is Top Kelly?"

The new sergeant didn't answer right away; he just stared at me. When he spoke, his speech was slow and thoughtful.

"You must be the kid the captain and Top Kelly were talking about."

The gunny had six rows of ribbons over the left side of his chest, and his eyes were boring holes through me. I had the same feeling the enemy must have felt when he faced them down—the urge to retreat was overwhelming.

The gunny continued, "According to your service record book, you're a little under five-ten, one-seventy, green eyes, and brown hair. Primrose, you don't look old enough to drive by yourself. If you have already served a four-year tour, you must have looked about twelve when you first enlisted. To be frank Primrose, you don't look like recon material to me, but your SRB shows you were a platoon honor man in boot camp, and honor men aren't chosen lightly! There must be something in you that doesn't meet the naked eye."

The gunny was turning the pages of my SRB and frowning, eyebrows raised. He was starched and creased from head to toe, and when he moved, his uniform never showed a wrinkle.

The gunny spoke again, "In the old Corps, Primrose, we had a lot of men who looked like boys and fought with a furiousness that belied their appearance; I hope you are of the same breed!"

I answered, "I'll try and live up to the high standards set by Marines before me."

"My name is Gunnery Sergeant Vicks. Top Kelly is on emergency leave, and he left all your papers with Captain Erndt. The captain has decided to give you a chance, if you can pass the physical. The captain was not all that excited about your intentions, but the Corps needs men, and whichever way your training goes, the Corps wins. You're scheduled for your physical today. Report back here in the morning at 0800 for the results. If all goes well, you'll be on your way to Pendleton in a couple of days."

The following day I reported back to the old, two-story building, and Gunny Vicks led me into the captain's office, where I signed the re-enlistment papers. Captain Erndt and the gunny wished me well as they handed me the manila envelope with my orders to Pendleton. Enclosed in the orders were a plane ticket to San Diego and a bus ticket from there to Oceanside, California, where there was Marine transportation to Main Side Pendleton. Camp Pendleton hadn't changed since my last tour of duty, where Staging Battalion was the home for all Marines heading overseas.

CHAPTER 2

Camp Pendleton

The Marine bus stopped at Division Headquarters, and most of the passengers dismounted and headed for personnel with their orders in hand. The office poughs handled everyone in their ever-so-efficient manner, and before long all the newbies were heading for their new commands.

After a brief look at my SRB, personnel discovered my old military occupational specialty and with Recon School a week out, thought I should head over to G-2 and use my skills and experience to become a Remington raider once again. I tried to look on the bright side of the typing assignment: I would have access to classified material, which might help on my search-and-rescue mission. I had in the past worked in the Cryptographic Section at Barstow Supply Center and hoped someone from there might be at Pendleton and could give me a hand.

After reporting in, I spent the rest of the day getting new uniforms from supply, obtaining my quarters assignment, and walking my SRB to the right people. The next day I would report to G-2 for my six days of torture. Because I'd kept my old uniforms, I didn't stick out as the new guy. The Corps in all its wisdom allowed me to keep my old rank of E-4, which kept me off head duty.

Being in the transit barracks was a plus because nobody really knew what to do with people in limbo, waiting on orders or movement. Just trying to keep them busy was about all that could be managed. In my case sending me to G-2 was easy; I would be out of their hair for a week.

When I reported in at Division Headquarters the following morning, a smart ass BAM (broad-ass Marine) decided to make my life miserable. She informed me that being in transit didn't give me license to be a slacker. I told her my assignment was in G-2, with some Crypto stuff, but she just laughed. The BAM was plump and nasty, with ugly teeth. On her best day she couldn't get anyone to take her to a fast-food restaurant.

A warrant officer, fourth grade came into the office while I was sparring with the dateless BAM and asked if the temporary typist had shown up. The BAM didn't smile, but gave me a dirty look, then pointed me out and waddled away. The gunner (CWO-4) said to follow him, there was someone who wanted to say hello from the old days at Marine Corps Supply Center, Barstow. We walked into the office down the hall, and behind the desk stood a major who had been my boss at Repair Battalion, MCSC, Barstow.

"Hello, Corporal Primrose! It's been two years since our last meeting. I want to thank you again for pulling me along during the running part of the inspector general's physical fitness test. If I hadn't made the time limit, my fitness report would have been suspect. Why did you re-enlist?"

"Well, Major Crowder, it's a long story. Could we talk about it in private sometime?"

Major Crowder replied, "Sure, let's meet after work today. In the meantime, I have a pile of typing for you—you ready?"

"Yes sir, but I may be a little rusty. Civilian life had me dealing blackjack and racking pipe on a drilling rig. It'll take a little while to get tuned up."

"The pile of papers I have for you is of a sensitive nature and for your eyes only. Your memory will go away every day at 1600."

"Yes sir, I understand, Major Crowder." With that, the major led me to a desk, on which sat a basket marked IN and piled high with papers. The major walked away, saying, "Get going in duplicate."

All the papers were stamped TOP SECRET. I had seen this kind before on Okinawa, with Third Motors. We typed stuff like this for a lieutenant colonel who worked on logistics problems facing motor transport companies in South Vietnam.

As I fought my way through the box, I ran across a message about a possible sighting of civilians in Laos. This could be a little ray of sunshine on my search. I noted the sighting was old by today's standards. The discovery hadn't drawn much attention and was buried at the bottom of an extensive report by a long range reconnaissance patrol mission into Laos.

The sighting was made by a Special Forces team in an area they were not supposed to be in, so naturally the report didn't pinpoint their exact position. The patrol had been somewhere in northern Laos, not far from the border with South Vietnam. The team was on a search-and-rescue effort for a downed pilot; while combing the area, they ran across a rest and relaxation compound for the North Vietnamese Army and Viet Cong officers, and that's where the civilians were spotted.

Not finding the pilot and not wanting the enemy to know they had discovered the R & R compound—in case intelligence wanted to keep it under surveillance—the LRRP made a stealthy retreat back into

South Vietnam. The Special Forces leader reported they had observed a tall blonde and two round-eyed men and couldn't believe their eyes. He added the trio could have been made up to look that way. The exact coordinates were not reported, just the general area logged in by a Captain Higgins.

I stored Higgins in my memory banks for future reference, hoping he would still be in-country when I arrived. If he had rotated back to the world, then he would be a lot harder to locate and talk to. If he could remember the coordinates of the compound, I could walk right in and not have to spend a great deal of time on recon. I was hoping the trio was entertaining the troops and would continue until the cavalry arrived.

I typed until 1600. The gunner left, and Major Crowder said, "Well, Primrose, let's have it."

When I explained my situation to the major, he said, "I've heard of the abduction, but I don't know any more about it than you do. I'll try and pull some strings to see what's out there and find out about any updates."

We talked some about old times at MCSC Barstow. Before leaving the office for the day, Major Crowder told me he was being rotated to Vietnam, via Camp Hansen, Okinawa, and that he would keep track of my whereabouts.

"Primrose."

"Yes, Major."

"Please keep all the things we talk about under your cover; some of the information we'll be looking into is on the sensitive side."

"Yes sir."

I thanked Major Crowder, and we departed for the day.

#

It was a long five days in the Crypto Section. I had tons of typing, and no more information on the trio came across my desk. For five days the fat-ass BAM corporal did her best at being an arrogant bitch. It appeared to be her sworn duty to make my days as miserable as hers; thank God she didn't out rank me!

On the fifth day I was informed my recon class started the next morning. I was glad to leave all the typing shit behind. The only good thing was the small bit of information about the trio and the name of the captain who knew where the NVA compound was.

From what I'd heard about recon training, the BAM corporal would be an angel compared to the instructors there.

CHAPTER 3

Recon Training

When I reported in at recon the following morning I got the feeling some very unpleasant experiences were about to descend upon me. The formation was full of wanna-be's, and a very ugly, disagreeable first sergeant was there to greet us. He was a big man, with meat hooks for hands and scars from head to toe. According to him the scars were from combat. By the look of his nose and eyebrows, he had once been a practitioner of the "sweet science," and I guessed he had never lost a fight.

Old grumpy looked us over and decided we were pale, overfed, lazy, fat, first-class pukes. He thought the Corps was scraping the bottom of the barrel for recon material, and he came down on us with a fury we hadn't heard or seen since boot camp. Then he yawned and said he should see a shrink for agreeing to train such a lowly group of shit-birds. Sergeant Ugly had decided our lily-white, soft-ass lifestyle would get us zapped by the hard-core jungle fighters in the bush very early in our tours. His next cherry statement was that even if he did his best and we did our best, we would all die the first week in combat.

Then the sergeant did a one-eighty and went on to say if we trained exactly as he instructed and performed as directed, we could defeat the enemy on any terms. Then he took a second look at the group, shook his head and said, "Nah, you guys are lower than whale shit. You'll never make the first week in the bush."

The first sergeant's name was J. B. C. Hills, and he was from Montana. He was not a prejudiced man; he hated everyone and everything on the planet. Hills was now ready to share his love for violence with his new enemies: we, the poor souls under his guidance.

First Sergeant Hills's reputation preceded him, and it said he was the right man to teach us to kill the enemy and survive in the hostile, war-torn jungles of Vietnam. His final words before the hell of his training were "If you people will keep your collective heads out of your collective asses, I may be able to teach you enough to survive at least a week."

We received training in weapons; explosives; scuba; jump school; and navigation, land, and sea. That not being enough, there was map reading, native languages, first aid, and small boat operations. There was sleep deprivation, which was the hardest: trying to think rationally when totally exhausted is a real trick. Then it was run up the hills, back down the hills, around the hills—day and night were the same.

The ugly first sergeant beat all our asses. Running, walking, climbing, or shooting, it made no difference to him: he was an iron man for sure, and we were lucky to have him as our mentor.

After six grueling weeks we were pronounced fit to carry the pack of a recon Marine. One of the lessons learned from the old salt was STEALTH and PATIENCE. The main goal of recon, gathering information and then melting away, never to be seen or heard, was drilled into our skulls. Engagement was an option, and we were well prepared for that scenario, along with the ability to take out certain targets of opportunity when called upon.

The first sergeant hadn't changed his mind; he still thought we wouldn't last the first week in the bush, but he shook our hands and wished us well. One of the guys asked him what the initials J. B. C. stood for. He laughed and said, "Just B. Cool." And then the ugly old First Sergeant Hills turned and walked away to another group waiting to get a taste of his measure.

When the class was called to attention and we marched over to the six-by transport trucks, Sergeant Hills could be heard, "Would you ladies please come to attention? You people are by far the sorriest-looking group of pussies I have ever seen in all my days in the Corps—you won't last a week in the jungles of South East Asia."

After graduation from Recon School, I was ordered back to Camp Hansen, Okinawa, where I had gone to Personnel Administration School four years earlier, only this time I was going for processing and orientation prior to being shipped to I-Corps and the Third Marine Division.

CHAPTER 4

Okinawa, Japan

I reported to Camp Hansen and its processing center with visions of South Vietnam and my quest, but Murphy appeared again with some office puke, the kind I was trying to avoid, who decided that because I could type, had experience with Crypto, and hadn't been assigned just yet, he needed my services more than Recon. My updated q-clearance was becoming a pain in the ass. All this delaying caused by taking one lousy typing test in boot camp—would it never stop? After two weeks of the typing shit, a lieutenant colonel in charge of the section called me into his office—not a good sign for a lowly corporal!

#

Rhonda's plight was not getting any attention from the good guys. My thoughts of her beautiful face, long blonde hair, and the happy twinkle in her eyes were overwhelming. Her gorgeous figure, so nice to hold, brought back memories of the wedding day at the Little Chapel of the West at the south end of the Las Vegas Strip and a little water to my eyes. The night before the wedding, watching her perform at the

Black Magic Club, was a warm memory. Remembering the tall blonde singing a sultry song while playing the bass in the dimly lighted club brought chills to the spine.

Rhonda's choice to be a musician in the local night clubs and hotel lounges didn't fit the Catholic high school choir teacher's vision for her, but there was talk that she had come to watch, dressed in the fashions of the day. She didn't know Rhonda danced in Minski's Follies in Seattle at the World's Fair, and if she had, chances are she would have dropped over dead.

Meeting Rhonda when she was in the ninth grade was a heart stopper and love at first sight on my part. What she ever saw in me, only she can say. What I first saw in her still burned and each day I was set back from my quest made the burning go deeper. Thoughts of the way she might be treated by her captors made my blood boil, and the feelings of urgency were overwhelming.

"Corporal Primrose." I heard the colonel calling my name, and it brought me back to the real world from the warm thoughts of Rhonda and the clubs of Vegas.

"Corporal Primrose!" the colonel said again. "How about joining the present world here? The Corps has decided that because of your high expert rifle qualification, you'll be assigned to Scout Sniper School. The Corps needs snipers more than recon guys right now."

"Sir, I made a really cool deal when I re-enlisted and I thought since I held up my end of the bargain, the Corps should hold up its end," I retorted.

The colonel responded, "Sorry, Primrose, that's not the way it's gonna work. In its wisdom the Corps has decided you'll be a scout sniper and that's the way it is. Besides, your recon training will come in handy with the Scout Sniper School."

Being a good Marine, I retreated out of the colonel's office. Shit! One delay after another! It wasn't easy putting a good face on what I thought was a bad situation, so 1 decided to look at the positive and remember that snipers had a lot of freedom in the bush, even more than recon, so aside from the additional delay, it might turn out for the best. I thought to the Jack Mont Trio, "Hang on, these setbacks must be for a reason." Maybe the gods were on my side and directing traffic for me.

I never thought I was that good with a rifle, but if the Corps thought so, who was I to say? It was a cinch all my training would play a role in the eventual outcome, and with sniper time in the bush mostly unsupervised, I'd have time to snoop and poop for the trio. With the Third Division Sniper Platoons up north near the DMZ and close to Laos, it was as if an unseen wind was blowing in my sails!

Once I had found the trio—alive, dead, or mistreated, it wouldn't matter—there would be hell to pay. Someone was going to get their asses delivered on a platter to their god below—about six feet should do it. Damn, I wished I were there now!

There were a couple of things I needed to do while on Okinawa, so getting that done before Scout Sniper School was my next move.

Finding my cousin John Glass, who was stationed with Amphibious Tractors, was the first move. Gunnery Sergeant Glass was married to my blood cousin Lorraine. He was a China Marine from WWII, who had served in Vietnam as an advisor with the French—guess they didn't listen.

I located Gunny Glass at the Staff Non-Commissioned Officers Club a little after happy hour started, but being a lowly corporal, I could only stay a few minutes as a guest, so we shook hands and headed into the village outside the camp gate.

Gunny Glass chose a quiet bar and then paid the bar girls to leave us alone while I told him my story.

The gunny listened to me, then suggested I was two bricks short of a load and thought I could get a Section 8 (insane) no problem. We both laughed, and then I told him I was as serious as a drill instructor on inspection day.

When I told him the approximate area I wanted to search, he retorted, "I remember that area from the old days with the French. It was hilly, thick jungle, slippery mountain trails infested with the enemy. I suppose it hasn't changed much on all accounts. Your best bet would be to chopper in as close to the border as possible, then hump it. Or maybe forget the whole thing and let division handle it! But you won't will you?"

"No, as soon as I can get things together, I'll be on my way, reaching for the brass ring the first go around."

The gunny, being a good Marine and cousin, said he would head over to Regimental HQ and look for photos of the area, along with any updates from across the border. I asked the gunny, "Are you rotating to Nam?"

He responded, "No, been there, done that—along with Korea and WWII—which means I'm too old for this shit. You don't need my help on the ground, you need a bunch of dumb fuckers like you, but if there is anything I can do on this end, I'll be happy to lend a hand."

We downed a couple of beers, and I wished him well. Had he been younger I could have used some of his jungle experience and common sense. A Marine with combat experience from three wars would be one very valuable commodity. As I watched him walk away, I thought he must have some memories. He was right when he said, "Been there, done that."

The other thing I had to do on Okinawa was return a favor to an old papa san. I had promised the old man some pictures of his grandson.

While I was with the Third Motor Transport Battalion, located at Camp Schwab, myself and two other Marines had coached a Little League baseball team located across the island in a little village called Nago.

Because of President Kennedy's People to People program, we tried to be good neighbors and interact with the local population. The team pictures somehow got lost in the shuffle, so I had to hand-deliver the pictures to him myself.

CHAPTER 5

Nago, Okinawa

I borrowed a Mighty Mite jeep from Camp Schwab and drove over the mountain to the village of Nago and looked up the old man. I found him in the family burial ground, for he had passed a year earlier, so I dropped the pictures off at the mayor's office and asked him to post them for anyone who had been on the team.

There was one other thing in Nago that was on my agenda: Heto, the old man's nephew. Heto was a genius in the art of tracking and a master in the bush. He usually could be found in a little restaurant called Timikos, when he wasn't working for one agency or another of the US government.

Heto was the best jungle tracker in the world, and he worked at Camp Schwab when I was stationed there. He compared himself to the great Indian scouts of the old west and was my choice to lead the way through the jungle looking for the trio. Heto probably watched every cowboy and Indian movie ever filmed and would have fit in nicely in the 1800s.

When I walked into Timikos he was sitting at his favorite table by the back wall, facing the entrance. He never let anyone sit behind him or had his back to the entrance.

Heto stood up as I approached the table, bowed and bowed again as I returned his bow. This went on for about a minute before he extended his hand for a traditional Western handshake. All the bowing and handshaking over with, he asked, "What are you doing here, you left never to return?"

I didn't answer right away, but inquired about his family and how things were going for him. Heto was a man of few words, and had no comment, for he never spoke of his family. His father and grandfather were from the old school, both traditionalist karate instructors, and were not in favor of the modern world as they saw it. Heto was a martial arts instructor for the Recreation Department when I was stationed at Schwab, and—like his father and grandfather—he was very close mouthed.

When we finally sat down, he ordered some beer, and we talked of old times. He had contracted some work with his skills in tracking with the US Army, Air Force, and Marine Corps, but complained it was a never-ending process to get paid. After a couple of beers, I told him the story of Rhonda and her trio missing in Laos. He was sympathetic and tried to skim over a bad situation for my sake, not wanting to tell me what he really thought the trio's chances were, especially Rhonda's. He just said she was probably having a very rough time of it.

I asked, "Heto, have you ever done any work in Laos or Cambodia?"

Heto retorted, "I have done work in both places for the CIA, but they were like the military, not good on their promises."

"Would you be interested is coming over to the area and helping me when the time is right?"

Heto responded, "Sure, I'll give it some thought. If the money is right I would consider it."

My answer was simple, "The money will be coming out of my pocket."

"In that case, Primrose, I won't be unreasonable, just for old time's sake."

We had a few more beers, and with the bowing back and forth repeated as before, I departed wondering how Heto could put away so many beers and maintain the appearance of total sobriety. As I was leaving Heto said, "Here is my card with a special number for you to call when you're ready. I have an apartment in Naha and have connections with the Air Force at Kadena Air Base; transportation is not a problem! Just leave a message, and I'll be on my way to Da Nang."

I replied with a bow and a handshake and didn't want to know what he had on the US Air Force, that he could order up transportation on a whim and find his way to Vietnam. Heto's stature belied his abilities. He looked scrawny and underweight, with black hair and eyes and bushy eyebrows—a true warrior in mind and spirit, on a five-foot-two-inch frame.

#

With that small mission accomplished, I headed back over the mountain to Schwab, wanting to get the jeep back before dark so I could clean it and keep the motor pool guys from sniveling. While washing the Mighty Mite, I was thinking about all the petty shit everyone complained about. Visions of what Rhonda, Fred, and Jack were going through made my problems pale. The anger was building up inside; with the frustrations from the setbacks at every turn, I began to think Murphy was taking up permanent residence on my team. I prayed the trio was safe and could hold out until my rescue mission got off the dime, and the green flag dropped.

The following morning I received my orders for Sniper School, and the next step in my journey was about to begin.

When I reported in as I had at Recon School, standing there to greet the newest rifle experts was the ugliest Marine I had ever seen. It brought back recent memories of another first sergeant named Hills. I thought Hills from recon was ugly, but he looked like William Holden compared to this one—and not only that, he was a monstrous SOB, with an attitude to match. I'm sure his mother, if he had one, only conceived one child. He looked like Olive Oyl with muscles, and no hair: a long neck, a ski-jump nose, huge shoulders narrowing down to a very small waist, and massive legs.

He was around six feet in height, with long arms and enormous hands to choke you with. He yelled that from his point of view, as of that moment, we were whale shit. Sergeant Ugly Number Two said he wanted to take life insurance out on each and every one of us, because after our first week in the bush he would collect a million.

How did I get so lucky, to meet two of the ugliest sergeants in the Corps? Where did personnel find these guys?

Sniper School was similar to Recon, with a lot more shooting. Shoot, shoot, and shoot some more, with the bolt-action Remington the weapon of choice. It would hit whatever you were good enough to sight in, and it was usually more rifle than we were shooters.

In our training we learned to be invisible in any environment, to lie still forever, breathe very little, and remember every detail we observed. We learned to judge the weather from zero to a thousand yards out, to know windage and elevation, when to take the shot, and how to survive after the shot. It was revealed how a two-man team could pin down a whole regiment.

I really enjoyed Sniper School, even with the ugliest sergeant running my ass down at every opportunity. Just as before, we were considered the worst group of nerds anyone had seen in a generation. The group survived his torture and became better Marines and very good shooters, thanks to his training philosophy and dedication to make us or break us.

When graduation time came around, the first sergeant passed out our certificates declaring us scout snipers. The sergeant was happy we could hit our targets at over a 1,000 yards; he thought if we being so green were any closer, the bad guys would have us for lunch. Along with graduation came our assignments, which had us all in I-Corps and good ol' Primrose with the 3rd Division, which was up where I wanted to be—closer to Laos and my quest for Rhonda. There was a burning inside saying, "Let's go, let's go," the sooner, the better.

Everyone, with orders in hand, headed for their new duty stations. Except me, because the people in Crypto wanted some additional typing out of my ass. You'd think they would have a typing pool, and not drag everyone who can man a Remington into their original and two-copy world! I suppose getting on my way was not in the cards just yet.

One week later, my orders came through for Vietnam and the 3rd Marine Division, which meant I was finally on my way to actually get the ball rolling to find the trio. It was time for this Remington raider shit to stop, but I decided not to snivel or complain, because no matter how hard I thought I had it, the trio was sure as hell in a lot worse scenario. My heart skipped a beat when I thought of what could be happening to Rhonda.

#

I packed my sea bag and headed for Kadena Air Force Base to catch the first hop to Vietnam that had space available. I remembered the first time I had left the Rock years before by ship into friendly waters. This time I would be going by air into a very hostile environment, where a large contingent were dedicated to helping me find the happy hunting grounds. I knew I'd have every chance in the world to get myself killed, but I had a mission and nothing could be worse than being captured and in the same boat as Rhonda, Fred, and Jack.

With the constant purring of the engines on the jet plane, I slept, dreaming of rescuing my family from the clutches of the communist bastards.

No matter my mission, as soon as I had feet on the ground in Vietnam, the enemy would use all its cunning and skill to try and make every day my last; but I was better trained, highly motivated, and had right on my side. I didn't have to wonder whether I was going in the right direction: it was the only direction! I would be hard to kill, with my mission unfinished.

CHAPTER 6

South Vietnam

Being patient is hard when every day may be the last for the people you love, but patience would prevail until the mission was accomplished. All preparations had to be fine-tuned and in position before the move into an environment where death was a daily occurrence. My dreams of freeing the trio and kicking the shit out of their captors seemed almost real, like a premonition, a message to continue. I had the feeling I was being led through my dreams by a spirit guide, and awoke with a start, to find myself looking at Yankee Station off the coast of South Vietnam, with its sandy beaches, green canopy covering the jungle, and the red dust a'flying!

A six-by waited on the tarmac to take the new fucking guys to division HQ. When you're an NFG, you're tested by everyone who has been in-country for a while. Both those you bunk with and those who don't even know you will avoid you like the plague. NFGs usually get someone killed before they get tuned in and stop making rookie mistakes. The enemy, with the help of the thick jungle, makes the environment a very inhospitable place for the new as well as the old, so new fucking guys are continually tested by one and all until they prove themselves to be an asset.

I knew that my orders were for 3rd Battalion, 3rd Marines, so I had the driver drop me off there, before heading over to division. With sea bag in hand I entered the first tent I came to.

When I lifted the flap on the first tent it appeared Murphy was out of my hair, because it was the scout sniper platoon area and there stood my old friend, J. T. Martin. Martin was a corporal from the San Francisco Bay area. I was surprised to see him, because the last I had heard he'd had a run-in with a first sergeant and was doing soft time in Alaska. Martin was the rifle range record holder at Marine Corps Supply Center, Yermo, California, with the M14, so it was little wonder why he had been picked for scout sniper duty.

Martin looked at me. Then came the standard question, "What the hell are you doing here, Primrose? I thought you put in your time and were cooling your heels dealing blackjack in Las Vegas!"

I responded, "It's a long story. I'll tell you about it after I get squared away with battalion and company."

We talked a little longer, and then I made my way to battalion—a big mistake! I'd been in-country only an hour, and I was already in deep shit. The sergeant major and the gunny were both in my face at the same time, and the first sergeant joined in on the feeding.

The gunny bellowed, "Who the hell do you think you are?" I was told in no uncertain terms that I don't shoot the shit with the guys, or decide where I'll bunk or where I'll be assigned. The gunny continued, "You come to personnel first, and that's me! You got that, corporal? You were supposed to be with the others on the six-by, and because your dumb ass was not on the truck, you have been declared AWOL!"

I responded, "I knew where I was going to be assigned, and didn't want to schlep my sea bag all over the place. I figured to stow my gear and then report to battalion. Sorry about all the paper work."

Well, that didn't go over so good, and I got my ass chewed again by the sergeant major. He told me since I was an E-4 with four years service, I should show some semblance of intelligence, but so far he hadn't seen any. He accused me of getting my stripes by some administrative snafu, or by being mistaken for someone with an IQ way above my station.

The first sergeant asked me, "Where did you stow your gear, Corporal Primrose?"

"My sea bag is over in the scout sniper area." He smiled at me with a smile that meant I was about to be dumped on—big time!

Rubbing his hands together, he said, "What makes you think the Corps wants you to be a sniper? Just because you have special training, it doesn't mean that's where the Corps wants you to serve. I see from your SRB that you have one hitch as a 0141, battalion level administrative clerk, is that correct, Corporal?"

"Yes, Top, that's right, but that was supposed to go away with my additional training."

"Well, it hasn't gone away; also I see you have a top secret clearance from the Atomic Energy Commission."

"Yes, that's correct, I worked for them in the Nevada Desert."

"Good, Corporal Primrose, that's settled. You're assigned to the Crypto Section at battalion as of right now. You want to know why?"

"Yes, I'd like to know why, and at the same time request a transfer to the scout sniper platoon. Why waste my additional training?"

The sergeant major spoke up, "Don't be in such a hurry to get yourself killed, young man. There is plenty of time for you to go into the bush and let the enemy give you the ultimate test of your newfound skills. The reason your services are needed is because the Marine you will be replacing wanted to get some bush time and went out on a search and destroy mission and the score was eleven enemy dead and one friendly casualty. Guess who the friendly was! The billet you are to fill will require that you do not put yourself in a position where you could be shot, knifed, bombed, or captured. The info up in your pea brain will be of a sensitive nature, and it will stay in your head—from what I see so far, there will be plenty of room."

The first sergeant dropped the next bomb: "You'll report to division Crypto School for the next two weeks. There will be no side trips. Do we understand each other, Corporal Primrose? If not, we can go up and see the major!"

"I understand, Top!"

"Now get the hell out of my office, and give thanks that you're not sitting in the brig for your stupid, dumb-ass attitude. We'll see you back here in two weeks."

#

Another delay, Jesus! I entertained thoughts of going AWOL, finding Special Forces Captain Higgins to confirm the coordinates to the camp, and mounting a single-handed rescue mission. If Rhonda were still alive, how much time did she have left? Here I was fucking around going to schools, and not getting down to the business of getting organized for the search. That was burning too much daylight. My emotions said go, my head said be patient and get your ducks in a row. What's that the Boy Scouts say? Be prepared! My burning desire needed to be tempered with reason!

Would the curse of the 0141 shit ever end? All these delays because of one lousy typing test way back in San Diego. All I wanted was to find my wife and get her to a safe harbor, but it seemed I was destined to be distracted at every turn.

Could it be there was a good reason for the most recent delay, which allowed me to work in Crypto, where all the secret shit is stored? There would be ample opportunity to run across something about the trio. Could it be the gods were really on my side, guiding me with an unseen hand?

Two months back in the Corps, and I was getting a well-earned reputation as a maverick. But—reputation or not—the Corps, hadn't seen anything yet, if I got bounced around much more. Well, back to school—shit!

CHAPTER 7

Cryptographic School

School or headquarters; it's all the same, just a lot of bodies pushing paper, typing, and in general running around like crazy people. All kinds of brass, so starched they could be used to cut cake. Stateside regulations strictly enforced—division was a real pain in the ass.

It was late when I checked in, Lieutenant Pool, the officer of the day, and the night-shift people the only ones around, and not happy campers. The OD was a very unpleasant fellow, whose rotation was only a month away. He had a short-timer's attitude and was doing all he could to stay out of harm's way for the remainder of his tour. Evidently he was on somebody's shit-list and was lying low—out of sight, out of mind.

Being a lowly lieutenant was not good for your health in this neck of the woods—or should I say jungle? Officers in the bush were the main target of every enemy gun, a priority for all NVA and VC fighters. Being the unpleasant fellow he was, the lieutenant decided to make my road as rough as his. At the time, he was of the opinion I shouldn't have bothered him at that hour and suggested I could have reported in before 1600 so he didn't have to deal with me. Not knowing what else to do with me, he thought sending me to the transit barracks for the night would get me out of his hair.

Lt. Pool had little hair, so getting me out of it was not a problem. He told me to get my ass out of there and report back at 0800. There was a lance corporal out front with the duty jeep to take stragglers over to the transit barracks, which weren't barracks at all, but a row of tents from another era.

My stomach was growling, so I entered the nearest tent, stowed my gear on the first available rack, and headed over to the late mess. Walking quickly out the rear of the tent, I stumbled over a body lying on the deck, half in the aisle and half under a cot. I said, "Sorry pal." Then as I was about to carry on, I took another look. The form on the tent floor looked familiar, so I dragged the body out from under the rack. He wasn't happy about the dragging and mumbled, "I'm looking for a bottle of sloe gin I stored here a couple of days ago. Would you please leave me the fuck alone?"

Then the body took a double take in the dimly lighted tent and said, "Is that you, Primrose? What the hell are you doing here?" As I was answering the same ol' questions, we shook hands and he forgot about the gin bottle and wanted to talk about old times and new times, so we headed for the chow hall. I gave the small body a first-hand report on why the hell I was here and what had happened over the last couple of years.

Corporal Patrick Thomas Knight had been a battalion-level office pinky at Third Motors when we were on Okinawa. Knight was in G-2 and I was in the next office, in Personnel Records. Knight's favorite drink was sloe gin. How anybody could drink that shit was beyond me, especially when he mixed it with 7 UP and Coca-Cola. It was a wonder he had any stomach left!

It was also amazing that Knight, who looked like a high school freshman, vertically challenged and with his weight barely topping 130 pounds soaking wet, had ever made it through boot camp. But you could never really tell by just looking at a man what he was made of inside. P. T. Knight had the ingredients to be a Marine in spades. Sitting in the mess tent for late chow, I asked Knight why he was still in the Corps and what his goal was for re-enlisting.

Knight retorted very slowly as usual. Picking his words carefully, he said, "I re-upped for a four-year hitch, to get transferred to CID, because I intend to get a degree in law or become a cop after my service. It's a family tradition for the Irish section of Chicago, to be cops or lawyers, so we can chase the Italians around."

"Okay Knight, so you're with Criminal Investigation Division, what the hell are you doing in the transit barracks?"

"Primrose, you ask too many questions. I'm here for a refresher course at Crypto School, because the Corps in all its wisdom had me in supply and then decided they needed my photographic memory in the Crypto Section, and the technology had passed me by."

Why the Corps had Knight in supply was a mystery to me, because Knight was better suited for snooping around and finding things, be it information, people, or objects. I was thinking how valuable Knight would be in my quest and pegged him for recruitment.

"Okay, Primrose, school doesn't start for a couple of days, so if you want, we can do some sightseeing. I have access to a jeep!"

"Sure Knight. I need to get acclimated to the heat and a feel for the country, and there are a couple of things I should do before we have our heads filled with all that Crypto shit. Have you met anyone else that was stationed with us at Camp Schwab, who might be able to help with my search for Rhonda?"

"Nope, you're the only asshole I have met from Schwab, Primrose."

#

While touring the next day, I explained in more detail my reasons for re-enlisting and the abduction of Rhonda and her father. Knight was amazed that I had agreed for Rhonda to make the trip to this hostile environment. I tried to explain how Rhonda's dad had been here the previous year without any incidents. He was a WWII combat veteran who had a nose for the unexpected. Fred thought he could see trouble coming and dodge the bullet, but he obviously hadn't seen this one.

At least with Fred and Jack both veterans, they would know what to expect from their captors. I asked Knight, "Maybe when we finish school, you could keep an eye out at Division Headquarters for any information about the trio?"

"Listen, Primrose, if I get any information on the trio, you'll invite me to become part of the mission, right?"

"Okay, Knight, you're on."

CHAPTER 8

Battalion

After two weeks of Crypto School, which seemed like six, I reported back to Battalion and Sergeant Major Kilpepper, who acted like it was our first meeting, which was hard to believe after the riot act he had given me when I first checked in. The sergeant major had had a colorful career, being a fighter pilot in WWII and Korea. He was one of the few that refused a commission and were labeled "mustangs"—enlisted pilots. Sgt. Major Kilpepper was on his last tour, with retirement being his next duty station. Could be with retirement looming, he had mellowed, and along with that displayed unexpected good humor in my case.

It appeared he didn't hold a grudge; his only words to me were "Primrose, report to Staff Sergeant Heath in the Crypto Section as quick as you can. Now get your ass over there!"

Being of sound mind and body, I reported to Sgt. Heath as quickly as ordered. Actually, I couldn't wait to report in and get to the files. I believed I might run across something on the trio. Sgt. Heath told me the desk by the window was now mine, and no longer belonged to the guy who got his only combat experience, Purple Heart, and escorted shipment home—all in one day. Sitting there, I wondered how this desk would treat me! I was going on a search and rescue mission into the same area where my predecessor had taken his last breath. It was my hope that things would go my way, and no one would get an early ticket home on my account.

The out box on the desk was empty and the in box full, so I started using the one skill I hated and didn't want to use. I was at it again, all because of a lousy typing test taken in boot camp just a few years ago. If I had only known!

CHAPTER 9

Company

There was too much brass at Battalion, which meant too many cooks, spoiling the soup. Being at company level allowed me to keep tabs on who goes where, when, and for how long. There was a chance I could weasel my way onto some missions in the bush with the scout snipers.

I was reminded at battalion not to put myself in any situation that could result in being captured, but down at company level no one had ordered me to stay put and not venture out into the bush. I didn't bring it up, and no one else did either. My friend J. T. Martin said he would take me out as his spotter once in a while if the timing was right.

#

One afternoon Corporal Martin and I were walking into his tent, and I noticed a guy walk by wearing the darkest glasses I had ever seen. They looked like welder's goggles. I asked J. T., "What the hell was that guy wearing over his eyes?"

Corporal Martin responded, "You best stay away from that guy along with the rest of the battalion, who are scared to even say hello to him. His name is Tom Toms and he's a certified Section 8. Tom Toms does whatever he wants, whenever he wants."

"Okay, Martin, I'm sufficiently spooked. Tell me his story; I may need more than one crazy SOB on the mission, and he could be a candidate."

"Well, Primrose, if you must—here it is. Tom Toms is an American Indian from the Northwest, someplace called Lummi Island in Washington State, near the Canadian border. He was assigned to Force Recon when he first got in-country, about four months ago."

"I see he's one big dude."

"Yes he is, Primrose. I think he's around six-three and two-twenty. On his first mission in the bush, he managed to get separated from his team for two weeks. After the first week, he was declared MIA and presumed KIA, which would be typical for an NFG. Then one day he walks into the company area, looking like he just finished a sitting for a recruiting poster, after being lost in the jungle for those two weeks.

"His version of being lost for two weeks was a little too far out there for anyone to take him serious. He says he slipped off the trail and slid down a small cliff while they were setting up for a night ambush the second night out. Toms claims it was so dark he lost his bearings and went the wrong way looking for the team. Because he was an NFG, that was not too far-fetched. As he puts it, he wandered around for two days searching for the team; they were doing the same, looking for him, but they never hooked up, so he headed south until he came to a small village. The village people sort of adopted him and helped him find his way back. That's his story. No one really believes him, but there's no way to prove any different, unless someone could find the village people he claims to have lived with. The company commander at the time was about to rotate to the world, and he didn't want to deal with it, so Toms fell through the cracks, and now nobody wants to challenge him and do all the paper work.

"Ever since he returned from the two-week period of being lost, he has worn a small leather pouch around his neck under his utilities. He never talked about it or let anyone touch it, except for one night when Toms and a couple of others from his company had a small disagreement with some Army dudes and his pouch was ripped off. One of the Army guys found the pouch and returned it the next day, but before he handed it over, he took a quick peek into the pouch. You won't believe what was in it, Primrose!"

"Okay, so I won't believe it—so what the fuck was in it?"

Martin had a very serious look on his face, but his posture betrayed his real feelings—he was about to burst out laughing.

"Three fingers and two ears, of human origin. Because the parts were so small, they had to be oriental. The Army dude who brought the pouch back to Toms made no bones about it and asked him straight-out where he got the body parts."

Tom Toms, being a good Indian, told the truth, and everyone knew Indians don't speak with forked tongue—that's white man's dilemma. The Army guy freaked out and ran to the battalion sergeant major, who in turn went to the CO. The next thing, they had Toms cornered in the battalion headquarters and ordered him to display the contents of the pouch and explain how those contents had come into his possession.

Toms once again, being a good Indian and not speaking with a forked tongue, told how he came by the body parts. "In 1961when my brothers were with a special unit doing recon work in what is now known as I-Corps, they somehow wandered into Laos by mistake, where they were not supposed to be under any conditions. While trying to find a way out, they ran into an NVA patrol, which also wasn't supposed to be in Laos. The unexpected meeting resulted in the brothers being captured, and the rest of the patrol escaped back into South Vietnam. As the story goes because the patrol of Marines killed over half the NVA unit, my brothers were tortured beyond belief before they were killed. When a team was sent in to find them, they captured a VC who was with the NVA when the torture and killing took place, and he sang like a bird to cover his own ass. He said the NVA did the dirty work on the brothers, and that the bodies would never be found.

"I got the information about the torture and killing from one of the guys on the search team. I vowed to get revenge when I was old enough to become a Marine and be sent to Nam. My commitment was to take the Indian ways and get payback tenfold. So at the time I was supposed to be lost, I wasn't. I was on a one-man hunt for the enemy and got five the first time out."

"Toms said he was going to keep it up until he was killed or rotated back to the world, whichever came first. When Captain Easy took over the company, he was going to get him a Section 8 and send him the hell out of the country, but after thinking about it for a while, he decided to let him go his own way. The captain didn't want to deal with the red tape, and if word had gotten out to the press there would have been hell to pay. Besides, the captain figured if Toms was out there killing the enemy—what the hell, that's what he was trained to do and got paid for, and besides he was good at it. So Captain Easy said fuck it, let Toms go where and when he wants. As long as he's killing the enemy, more power to him.

"Toms has three bags and is working on the fourth, with a new one coming from a guy who makes them in his state of Washington. This guy is a tribal shaman and the pouches are supposed to be sacred somehow. As to the dark glasses, Toms never goes out in the daylight without them, which keeps his eyes ready for his nighttime adventures—he can literally see in the dark! I feel sorry for the poor fuckers who don't see or hear him coming—he owns the night."

I asked Martin why Toms cut off ears and fingers.

"Toms told me the leader of the NVA who killed his brothers was a woman and he takes the ears of the women he kills and the fingers of the men. So now you know a little about Tom Toms, and that's not all there is to the crazy fucker!"

I thought this Indian could be an asset to my mission so I put him in the ready room in the back of my mind. I questioned Martin again. "Do you know Toms well enough to arrange a meeting so I could talk to him?"

Martin said he would ask, but reminded me that Toms was one weird SOB, and one never knew what he was thinking or what he would do.

"Tell Toms our situations are similar, only his is to search and destroy and mine is to search and rescue. He might find some satisfaction helping find my people, and maybe an opportunity to add to his pouch."

"Sure, Primrose. I just waltz up to ol' Toms and say, 'Hey Toms, a guy I know wants to go into Laos and find some people, you want to go?' Shit, Primrose, he'd probably cut my fingers off."

#

A few days later Martin said he had a mission to whack some NVA officer they'd spotted using the same trail for nearly two weeks, and I was welcome to come along.

Martin usually thinks with a good portion of his brain, unlike some of the thinking that has gotten me into trouble. He suggested I talk to the captain or the sergeant major about my real reason for being in-country. Martin thought I needed one of them on my team.

"You'll have to take a chance and let one of them in on your scheme, Primrose."

"Okay, I'll take your advice, Martin, and talk with the captain."

"Captain Easy would be my choice, Primrose; he seems willing to bend the rules if he thinks something has merit or logic. He's a throwback from the Old Corps, where adventure was the name of the game. His family was all Navy, his father an admiral and his uncle a captain, but he chose the Marines after the academy, to piss off the Blue Water sailors."

"Thanks for the information, Martin. I'll talk to him tomorrow, and I'll let you know if I can get away for a couple of days to join you in the bush. Oh, one more thing, Martin, about Toms; you said he sleeps all day and never goes outside in the daylight without glasses? This is for night vision, right?"

"Yeah, that's right."

"Well, I thought Indians didn't do shit at night; and I thought they took scalps, not fingers and ears!"

"Look Primrose, you have to understand this is one crazy SOB. I asked him about the scalping shit. Toms said that was all white-eye bull shit. He said his people were more civilized than white people."

"Thanks for the information. See you tomorrow."

I needed to get to know that Indian—my kind of Marine.

#

My desk was right down from the captain's office. I hoped coming clean with Captain Easy wouldn't be a mistake.

Being so close to his office, I could tell if he was in a good mood or not. When he looked approachable, I asked him if I could have a few minutes in private on a personal matter that needed attention right away. He said to come right over whenever it suited my schedule.

Knocking on the captain's hatch, I called. "Sir, Corporal Primrose, request permission to enter."

"What's so important Primrose, that you need my valuable time? Do you realize I could be at the O Club right now with my snoot in a gin martini, or I could be in the ville getting laid. But no—I'm here looking at you, and not one bit happy about it."

As the captain continued a colorful rendition of Captain Bligh, I began to think I had picked the wrong day for our little talk.

"Well Primrose let's get on with it. And it better be good, with you into my drinking time!"

Not knowing whether I should continue, I decided to go forth like a raging bull and take my chances. "Sir, before we begin, I would like our conversation treated like a confession."

"Primrose, if you need a shoulder to cry on, you came to the wrong place. The chaplain is a couple of doors down, and I can arrange a meeting no sweat."

"No sir, what I mean is, our conversation goes no further than this room, unless the course of events dictate otherwise."

"Yes, Primrose, you have my full confidence, on my mother's grave, okay? Jesus, get on with it."

"Sir, do you remember any reports on a missing trio of musicians, who were presumed captured some time ago?"

"Yes, I recall the reports, and at the time thought it was very unusual."

"Sir, my wife was a member of the trio, also her dad and a good friend."

"Jesus, Primrose, what the fuck was your wife doing in this hell hole? Why would you allow her to come here? You are certainly one dumb SOB, if I may say so!"

"With all that said, sir, it goes like this: The trio was on a Far East tour, from Hawaii to Nam and points in between." I related to the captain what I knew and what my intentions were.

"Sir, I have the coordinates an Army patrol reported of a camp where high-ranking VC and NVA do their R & R, and that's where the LRRP reported seeing the round eyes. The Army guys said the camp was untouched and ripe for the picking. It's my intention to put a team together and find my wife. I pray every night that she is alive and unharmed, and that I get there in time to rescue her from those scumbags. But Sir, there is a small problem with the whole affair—the camp is in Laos."

"Primrose, are you a fruit cake or what? Do you have any idea what a mission like that would entail? You're talking major logistics, troops, choppers, air cover with fast movers, and—least of all—permission! You're not going to get permission to go over the border into Laos, and if that was even possible it would have to come from Washington, from a place called the Pentagon. You're talking battalion or maybe even regimental level planning."

"Sir, I have a way to pull it off with just a few good men and a couple of choppers. When I get it all together, I'll lay it out for you. What I need now is a little free movement, so I can put things together."

"Primrose, I understand your wanting to rescue your wife and all, but don't you think division is a better choice to handle this?"

"No sir, I've already checked and they won't touch it, and I believe we'd have a better chance of finding them, because I'm motivated and division isn't. How about it, Captain?"

"Okay, Primrose. I'll give you three weeks to get this thing together. You keep me informed at all times. When you present your plan, I make the final decision, if it's a go or not. Do you agree?"

"Yes sir."

"So, Corporal Primrose, get the hell out of my face, you're into my cocktail hour big time. One more thing Primrose, if you do something stupid like getting yourself killed, captured, or thrown in the brig, I don't know you, understand?"

"Yes sir."

The captain retreated out the main hatch and headed for the O Club, yelling back, "You better find someone to help you who knows the bush and is willing to crawl through it."

It was time to get the ball rolling, do some serious planning, and find the Army patrol leader who saw the NVA R & R camp. If the Indian would sign on with me, he could recon the camp. His report would determine the next move.

If Toms verified the camp and its inhabitants, then the green light would be on and the rescue in full throttle. My next stop, Tom Toms's hooch, for it would be good to deal with him in his own element and have him as comfortable as possible when we talked.

I walked over to Martin's tent to ask if he would introduce me to Toms. He was reluctant at first, but after a little arm-twisting he agreed. I think Martin was getting the bug to go on the mission.

Darkness was just creeping over the camp when we approached Toms's digs; he was just heading over for late chow. Corporal Martin, being very polite, asked Toms if we could join him for chow. Toms replied, "Sure. Chow, here we come. What's up with you, Martin?"

Martin, again being very polite, said, "My friend Primrose just got in-country, and he heard you might be from the same area, somewhere up near the Canadian border. Primrose would like to compare notes with you."

"Sure."

Martin nodded and said, "Primrose, meet Tom Toms, wild and crazy Indian."

After the introduction, we headed for the chow hall to have a quick snack. Toms said he had a mission and asked Martin if he wanted to go along. Martin declined, said thanks, but no thanks.

While shoveling down the chow, it was discovered Toms and I had lived in the same area and had attended the same school, but different years. As Toms put it the red faces didn't hang with the white eyes, so our paths never crossed.

Soon Martin begged off for the night, claiming he had to prepare for a morning operation.

I had to come clean about the introduction and said, "Toms, I asked Martin for the intro for more than our being from Washington. I have an agenda you might be interested in, and the strange stories I've heard about you piqued my interest. But I guess that wouldn't be a surprise to you."

"No surprise, everyone thinks I'm a crazy fucking Indian. And they could be right, in a sense. I'm a wild ass Indian, but not crazy. I'm here to kill our mutual enemy, as many as possible. I just want to do it my way, and you've probably heard all about that."

"Yeah Toms, I've heard, and that's one of the reasons I wanted to talk with you. My agenda includes a special mission that you might be interested in."

Toms looked through me with eyes meant for an eagle and replied, "I'm always interested in something special, because every mission I do is special. What's so hot about yours?"

"Well, Toms, first of all, it's unauthorized and will be known only to those directly involved."

"You know, Primrose, everything I do here is unauthorized. I'm here for only one reason—to kill as many of those little fuckers as I can. I suppose you heard about my brothers and what the enemy did to them to make this personal. Tell me about your unauthorized mission, while we have a few minutes."

"Toms, a few months ago there was a report of a trio of musicians who were ambushed and taken prisoner. Did you hear about that incident?"

"No, don't have a clue."

"The trio is still missing, but there is hope from an Army LRRP that made a sighting of three round-eyed civilians a month or so ago. The major stumbling block is the sighting was in Laos, and I need someone to go into Laos and check it out.

"The sighting was in an R & R camp for NVA and VC, so it will be a tricky business to observe the facility and confirm the report. A complete reconnaissance of the camp and surrounding area will be needed. If you decide you want in, there might be a chance to enhance your pouch."

"Primrose, I get the feeling you aren't telling me the whole story. Why do you give a shit about some missing civilians in this scumbag war?"

"You're right, Toms I hadn't gotten to that part yet. The missing civilian musicians consist of my wife, her father, and their leader. It's personal for me, like your situation, with the only difference being I may have a chance to save them. This mission will be a search and rescue if they are still alive."

"Well, Primrose, I won't ask why you allowed your wife to be here, that's your business. But it sounds like you didn't think it through."

"So what do you think, Toms, you want in on this war party? I can get you a chopper ride to the border, and you'll have to hump it from there. Remember, we won't be authorized for anything we do—we'll be flying by the seat of our pants."

"The war party—as you call it, Primrose—sounds good to me, so you can count me in. I can put another feather in my bonnet for killing some more of those fucks! If your people are there and alive I can add yet another colorful feather. But it's been awhile, Primrose. Do you think there's a chance they may still be alive?"

"I don't know, Toms, but you'll be able to find out. I pray they are. I can have a chopper for you on two day's notice, maybe less."

"As I said, I'm in on anything unauthorized, because that's right up my alley, and saving some American lives would balance out the other chore I have."

"Well, Toms, I tell you what: I'll square things away with the captain, to account for your absence. He already thinks you are two scalps short of a belt, and I think he would like to see you disappear for more than a few days. I'll get back to you when I have your transportation lined out. And once again, Toms—I owe you big time."

"Think nothing of it white eyes. I relish snooping; that's what Indians do best."

So far on this little mission, all I had to do was get an unauthorized chopper to go on an unauthorized mission, deliver a certified nut case Recon Marine to a country off limits to our side, and get everyone back alive. Not bad for starters. No big deal right? Piece of cake!

There was a tugging in my gut to get things moving, and with every sunset the urgency increased. I could only imagine the daily hardships Rhonda was going through. I kept telling myself, Be patient. Get it right.

#

As a teenager I ran around with a group of kids who lived in the same trailer park and one of the girls had a younger brother who used to tag along. He was now in Nam with the First Cavalry, down south somewhere, flying a Huey. If I could talk him into flying up north, our first go around would be in the books. When I found Captain David Wilson Schroud, we'd talk of old times, and I'd try and get him to give us a hand and drop Toms off on the border with Laos.

While I was down south, I'd look up Capt. Higgins, the Army Special Forces team leader who had stumbled onto the camp where the trio was being held. I'd need a face to face with him, to get confirmation on the coordinates and a feel for the area, as Toms would be needing all the help he could get. My hope was that the captain was still in-country, and not rotated—or worse yet, killed in action!

When Toms committed to be my first team member, I headed over to the company office to speak with Captain Easy. "Sir, I request permission to head down south and visit the First Cavalry, where I have a friend who is a Huey pilot. I have a message to deliver to him from his family, and while I'm there I'll look up the LRRP leader who made the report about the trio."

"Primrose, take all the time you need, you won't be missed. I wonder why the Corps has spent all that time and money training you, because so far you haven't produced shit. From what I can see you are as useless as a pair of ice skates in a bowling alley. I hope you're a whole lot better in the field than you are in the office."

"Sir, as you know, I requested Recon only, not Scout Sniper or Crypto. I've volunteered to go into the bush anytime, but all I ever get is the Remington raider shit, and because of one lousy typing test in boot camp."

"Just go, Primrose, before I find a full in box for you!"

Before I departed for the First Cavalry, I called Schroud's folks and got an approximate location. Good news: he was flying for a general and not ducking too many bullets.

CHAPTER 10

Down South: First Cavalry

I located the First Cav O Club and wrangled a visitor's pass. As luck would have it, Schroud was at the bar, three sheets to the wind, bragging along with all the other wing-wipers about their flying expertise. Actually, luck didn't play much of a role. It was happy hour, and that's where all good pilots would be—at the bar, waving their arms in simulated combat.

Schroud looked about the same as he had in the old days hanging out at the local drive-in. He was brown and brown, five-ten, one-sixty, with a sneaky smile permanently registered on his face.

I tapped him on the shoulder and said, "Hey, I'd like to see the El Camino since you painted it!"

Schroud turned to see who was bothering him and stared for a moment, then turned back to the bar before whirling around to say, "Jesus, Primrose, you scared the shit out of me, like you were a ghost or something! What the hell are you doing here? You're supposed to be back in the good ol' US of A. I do believe a change in scotch is in order. What the fuck are you doing in uniform? It looks like you're back in the Corps. Didn't you get enough the first go-around?"

"It's a long story. If you can focus those eyes long enough, let's head for the dining room and have some chow and coffee while I explain my situation—which is very serious, by the way."

"Primrose, are you under the impression that I've had too many toddies to listen and navigate? I, my friend, have the ability to fly and drink with the best of them, which means the more I drink, the better I get."

I didn't smile, and said, "Like the older you get, the better you are?"

He got the message, and we headed for the dining room.

As Schroud was eating and drinking coffee, I told him I'd seen his family before I left the States. I mentioned his dad was his usual grouchy self, his mom still the Mrs. Cleaver on the block, and his sister working and enjoying life.

"Well, Captain, are you ready to listen, now that you're full of steak and coffee?"

"Sure. Fire away, Zach. What's so important that it would bring you to this ungodly place?"

"Do you remember hearing about a trio of civilian musicians who disappeared a couple of months ago?"

"Seems like I do recall something like that; so what?"

"The trio that came up missing and presumed kidnapped consisted of Rhonda, her dad, and their friend. It was called the Jack Mont Trio."

"Rhonda? What the hell! Her dad. Holy shit, Primrose, what the hell were they doing here? Has there been any word of them?"

"Nothing concrete, just a sighting by a Captain Higgins who was leading an LRRP team searching for a downed pilot. I need to locate him and ask about his discovery and what the coordinates are. The information I have collected so far is considered top secret. I only discovered it because I was working in the Crypto Section at Division Headquarters. It was dumb-ass luck to run across that report from Captain Higgins."

"Hell, Zach, locating the captain is not a problem, if he's still in-country. Is that all you wanted?"

"No, not exactly; when we get the coordinates, I'll need a chopper to deliver a Recon Marine as near the border with Laos as possible, then he can hump it in from there."

"Okay Zach—tell me how all this got started, for Christ's sake! Why the hell would you allow Rhonda to travel in these dangerous waters? Shit!"

"Well, it was an opportunity for her to make some money, get some free travel, and have a good experience. Since she was with her dad, I said okay."

"The next thing I know two black ops guys pay me a visit. One of the assholes did all the talking and informed me that Rhonda and her group were missing, presumed captured by enemy forces and being held for ransom. The jerk went on to say they were doing all they could to rescue the trio and expected to get a ransom demand for their release, at any time. By his attitude, I knew he was full of shit, could care less about the trio, and was just trying to keep it out of the press.

"So being of sound mind and body, I re-enlisted in the Corps and got myself assigned to the 3rd Marine Division. I just waded through a lot of shit to get this far, and the shit is getting deeper, I'll tell you about it sometime. After five minutes with the black ops guys, I knew Rhonda's only hope for rescue was by someone personally involved—me! So do you think you can give us a hand?"

"One thing, Zach; why don't you use Marine Air?"

"Shit, Schroud, I don't know any Marine pilots—and besides, one doesn't just go around asking pilots to appropriate a chopper and head out on an unofficial mission. I can't just round people up to do special missions. I'm a corporal, not a fucking general!

"This mission will be unofficial, not-known to anyone above my company commander. I'll need your bird for the first go-around, the second, and probably more. Everything we do will be off the record, illegal, dangerous, and totally secret from anyone not directly involved."

"Zach, I think what you're telling me is we could all wind up in Leavenworth or dead! Does that about cover it?"

"What we have here, David, is a group of men trying to do a job higher authority won't do. Because it's in Laos doesn't make it impossible. Are you up to it?"

"Hell, yes! Since I've been in-country, I haven't had my ass to close to the fire. Driving a general around is like doing soft time. A little adventure wouldn't hurt, especially helping Rhonda and her dad. Yes, I'm up to it. Whatever you need, Zach, just let me know—come to think of it, I have a little flight in a couple of days to a CIA ranch just inside the border with Laos. I'm taking two general officers and a couple of bird colonels to a three-day ranch party.

"There'll be booze, broads, and steaks, which means I'll be sitting on my ass for three days. Driving for a general means I have a lot of freedom of movement and don't need an excuse to be in any certain area. I can drop you guys off no problem. Along with that, there's a milk run up north in your area I do every three days. I go up north to trade some hard-to-get items for items harder to get, if you know what I mean! Being a dog robber for the general has its benefits, like trading medical supplies for some good steaks and booze. The Navy has the best chow, which they steal from the Seabees who steal it from the carriers, who steal it from the submariners. Voila! Steaks for an army general. I'll let you know when I can pick up your Recon guy. It'll be a morning departure and an evening drop off—should be a piece of cake!"

"Now with that out of the way, how do we find Captain Higgins?"

"Zach, go over to the EM Club and cool your heels for a couple of hours. I'll locate Higgins, if he's in-country."

#

I wandered over to the Army Enlisted Club. It was a paradise— compared to the clubs up north, it was almost like being stateside. I hung out for a couple of hours and had a steak dinner and a few beers, trying to stay out of trouble, being the only Marine in the joint. I had some serious looks, but no trouble. Schroud came in at 1630 hours and said, "I've located Higgins. The captain is in the hospital from wounds sustained in a firefight a couple of weeks ago. Higgins said he would talk to you about his discovery. I have a jeep outside.

We found Higgins sitting outside the entrance to the hospital, in a window seat, smoking a very smelly French cigarette, long and thin. He just nodded when we walked up and Schroud introduced us.

Captain Higgins had been told to keep his mouth shut about finding the camp, but after Schroud explained the situation, he had no problem telling everything he knew or was asked. Higgins gave the coordinates and said they were right on, and the civilians he had seen were as he said—a tall, blonde woman and two round-eyed men.

Higgins repeated, "It wasn't hard to tell they weren't part of the little fuckers crowd; it didn't take a second look, and we didn't have time for that anyway. Getting the hell out of there without detection was priority number one. I wish you well, my friend, and please forget you ever saw me. If things go bad for you, I don't want to be involved."

The captain limped away, waving adios. Higgins was not a cheerful fellow at the moment, and I guessed when you're recovering from your third Purple Heart, you kinda have a sour outlook on life. He was really one of the genuine heroes. Captain Schroud pulled me into the jeep, saying, "Come on Zach, the chopper is waiting."

CHAPTER 11

Up North: 3rd Marine Division

The trip back up north was uneventful. Schroud dropped me off on the tarmac and said to have the Recon guy ready on very short notice. Schroud added, "I'll drop the guy as close to his objective as possible."

With that said, he was ready to lift off, but not before loading a couple of cases of scotch, which had been traded for some condoms and mouthwash. Watching the exchange led me to believe that nothing moved in-country without some kind of deal in the process.

I headed back to the area looking for Toms, but thought waiting until dark would be prudent. I didn't want to piss the Indian off before we even got started. My next move was to find Martin, but that was a no-go either.

One thing for sure, I'd go with Martin next time he went into the bush and try to get in some kind of shape for my own mission.

Just before dark I found Toms sitting by his rack, using his footlocker for a table to clean his Colt .45 and M-1 Carbine. Not far from his reach were a couple of very sharp and deadly looking knives, made by KA-BAR from a special design submitted by Toms—the master knife fighter and meaner than a junkyard dog!

Without looking up Toms said, "Hello, Primrose. When do we get this war party on the road?"

"Toms, your ride could show up with little or no notice at any time, beginning at 0600 tomorrow, so you need to have all your gear ready and waiting."

"No problem, I'm ready right now and will stay ready from now on. This evening I'm heading into the night, hoping to finish filling my pouch and begin the new one I received last week. Do you believe in fate, Primrose? I do. It was fate that brought us together, I can feel it. Indians feel things you white asses don't. Something big is coming out of this powwow of yours, Primrose. I know it. I feel it—bet on it! Let me know when the bird will arrive—I'm ready."

With that said, Toms walked out and vanished into the night, to find and confront the enemy on his terms, and I felt sorry for the poor fuckers he would be putting his blade to. The enemy would never know what happened; one minute alive and well and the next in the happy hunting grounds, wherever that was for them. My only hope was that Toms didn't make a mistake and get himself killed before we got the mission underway.

If there was ever a Marine in the right place at the right time, Toms was that Marine.

The next morning, I headed over to the company office. After checking in, I found a note from Captain Schroud: "Package pickup, noon tomorrow."

The first shirt gave me the rest of the day off, so I walked over to find Toms. He had just come in from the bush, with a broken arrow. Broken arrow meaning the great Indian hunter strikes out on a hunt. Two had slipped away from him and getting him to tell how they got away was like pulling teeth. It came out very slowly.

Toms spoke slowly, "Being a great warrior, silent and brave, my dumb ass stumbled over a trip wire a blind man could see. Tins cans went off all over the place because of my stupid mistake. It won't happen again. I did manage to leave my calling card, which has a spear and knife crossed at the middle, with a chief's headdress above and a bow below. At the bottom of the card is a straight arrow for my signature. I want them to know who is hunting them!"

I told Toms that the calling card would surely get a huge bounty on his head and probably surpass some of the higher ones on the scout snipers. He enjoyed the idea of a large bounty and vowed to do better in the night and thought his red ass should have the highest bounty in-country.

"Primrose, I want to be a magnet for the NVA and VC to come to, which means I won't have to go tramming all over the fucking jungle looking for them."

"Toms, you are a sick puppy. Your ride will be here at noon, so be on the tarmac at 1130 hours."

"No problem Kemosabe."

It was impossible to see Toms's eyes with the dark glasses, so trying to read him was almost impossible, except for his posture and hand motion when he talked.

With lots of time on my hands, I walked over to the tarmac to wait for Captain Schroud to land for Toms's pickup. The chopper was on time, but Schroud had some business that would take about three hours to complete, so he said to hang loose and have Toms stand by.

The chopper captain's business was trading gold for medical supplies that were all black market; it required a certain amount of finesse to keep all parties involved happy. The goods were located in an old warehouse, near a very seedy part of town. Taking his whole crew was a prudent move—you never knew when the shit was going to hit the fan.

Toms, not letting three-hour delay bother him, sacked out on the tarmac and was asleep in five minutes. Three hours would pass quickly for him, but for me it was find some shade and worry about all the things that could go wrong.

When Schroud and his crew returned, they were excited and soaked to the skin with sweat. The trade had gone bad from the beginning.

In an agitated tone, Captain Schroud explained, "When we entered the warehouse, the guy we had done business with was hanging from the rafters, with a western style noose around his neck. He had a note pinned to his chest written in English, 'Whoever traded with this asshole will suffer the same fate!' At that point we started to retreat out of the building, but it was too late—we were surrounded.

"Their leader stepped forward to announce he was the new proprietor, and any deals would go through him. He pointed to the stiff hanging from the rafters, and the meaning wasn't lost on our little trading company. We made our first trade with the new guy: our lives for a little gold and no medical supplies."

Schroud said one of these nights when the warehouse was full of supplies and people, he would have a couple of gun ships level the place. The message would be clear. You don't fuck with the First Cav.

When the chopper was ready for liftoff, I woke Toms and got him aboard. Then I told Schroud Toms thought it would take three days for his recon and I'd give him a heads up for his extraction, which should be about the same time as his regular milk run. They lifted off in a cloud of red dust, heading for the border with Laos.

CHAPTER 12

Laos

Sitting in the chopper and feeling the vibrations from the rotor blades made me think of eagles. Here I was soaring like an eagle, feeling the wind blow through the hatch, but not feeling like an eagle. Maybe in a past life I was an eagle. I'll have to ask the shamans: they know about such things, they are sensitive to the past and future. When I get back to the world I just may study to be a shaman for my tribe, and then attend to some things that need attention on the reservation. One thing for sure, the chopper ride beats the shit out of tramming through that thick-ass jungle below. I believe the eagle has the right idea—stay aloft as long as possible before you dive on your enemy or prey below.

The door gunner tapped me on the shoulder and motioned we were over the drop-zone, and then he handed me a map, which pinpointed the exact location of the landing zone. I suggested he take the chopper in a little closer, but that was a negative. When the pilot started to hover, the gunner threw a rope out the hatch and motioned me to find my way to the ground via the rope. No way was he going to get any closer to the green jungle canopy. Being a good Boy Scout, I hit the hatch and slid down the rope to the thickest jungle I had ever encountered. Finding my way through the canopy to the jungle floor was like diving into a bowl of pea soup.

Not only was the canopy thick, the jungle floor was like a ripe cornfield, ready for harvest, where you could see about as far as you could reach. I was thinking Primrose had gotten me into something I might not like, and I might have to take a finger or two from his ass! Working in the daylight was a serious pain in the ass, but no way around it; besides, it was almost as dark on the jungle floor as late evening. As the ol' drill sergeants would say, I'd have to improvise. It was getting late, so spending the night here was a real possibility. As much as I would rather travel through the night, I needed to mark my trail for the return trip, and daylight was best for that. Even in daylight hours, visibility was limited in this viscous weed patch, which had less light than the inside of a salmon. All things considered, the low light was good for my night eyes, so the sniveling had to stop.

I found the crotch of a good-size tree, where my red ass could spend the night and hope no small or large critters screwed up the R & R while I dreamed about being back home on the reservation, fishing, hunting, and exploring Lummi Island, feeling the cool breeze coming off the straits and blowing through the trees, the current warm for swimming and a little fufu with the local maidens!

While setting up a defense for the night, I was thinking there were six months left in-country and one more year at Pendleton, before heading back to the reservation. Getting home would be followed by going back to school in Bellingham and getting a law degree. Then to the reservation police, and a run for judge. A future chief needs to be educated in the ways of the white man. Being third in line for chief was not a problem until my dumb-ass brothers got themselves killed and made me first in line. They left all the chief shit up to me—thank you very much!

With chief staring me in the face, I believe a name change would be in order. Being introduced as Tom Toms brings up images of Indians dancing around a fire to the beat of tom-toms, getting fired up to attack the fort defended by John Wayne.

I think I'll change my name to Tom E. Fingers, attorney at law. It would be fitting, as Fingers would be a good Indian name. According to stupid white man's legend, Indians used to name their newborns for whatever they saw at birth. Like Sitting Bull, Dead Bird, or Tepee—what a crock. I'll enjoy hearing my new name, Tom E. Fingers, spoken aloud, knowing the real reason behind the name, which will remind me of the warpath I followed while in the shit hole of Nam.

#

The sounds came and went, and I finally realized I wasn't dreaming. It was 0600. The canopy above and floor below looked like the inside of the Jungle Club in Honolulu. I couldn't see shit—me, the Indian who can see in the dark. This was my reward for going out in the light of day and ruining my night vision with light blindness. The canopy hanging overhead was like a huge cloud, with little rays of sunshine peeking through. One good thing the filtered light showed was that the jungle floor was not so cluttered as I had thought, so walking wouldn't be difficult. Time to go!

Leaving a good trail would be prudent, for coming out, chances were I'd be on the double with no time for a compass. Compasses don't work around me so good anyway, with my magnetic personality confusing the needle.

After a three-hour trek through the jungle, I stopped for a reading. My personality must have taken a powder, for the compass was working fine. I was standing at the exact coordinates the LRRP guy had given Primrose.

While I was looking at the compass, I stepped up to a small rise, which allowed me to see some very straight lines through the bush. There are no natural straight lines in nature, so the lines had to be manmade.

Trying to get a better look, my Indian ass stumbled forward and my eyes fell upon the compound we were searching for. The LRRP guy's numbers were right on the money; with a few more steps the perimeter fence would have been in my way. Jesus, here I'm the great Indian scout, tracker, hunter, and enemy killer, and I didn't even see the fucking fence!

If their security was worth a shit, I should be dead already! Taking a closer look at the area, I couldn't see any guards or towers—these little fuckers sure felt safe and secure. It was like they had their heads in the sand. I started following the fence, to locate the guard shacks and entrance, which was a high priority in order to count any traffic in or out.

It took me an hour to walk, crawl, and fight my way through the undergrowth and weed-infested fence line all the way around. I didn't see any roads, trails, or activity, but there had to be a way in and out, so I crawled around again, only this time more slowly. I spent more time checking for the telltale signs of camouflage. Being a good Indian scout, I'm supposed to find these things, no problem. Which is another white man's legend, like Tonto had just left the reservation when Hollywood called; he never spent five minutes in the woods or jungle. "Me Indian Toms, I good scout, Kemosabe, have plenty of bush time!"

Hell, there it was! I could see the faint tail of diesel smoke as I crawled right over a manmade bridge. No wonder there wasn't a lot of security; the place was indiscernible from the ground or air. A lot of time had been spent building this compound, and it wasn't new. I followed the road as it headed north for about a quarter of a mile and then passed between twin peaks.

The peaks were to the north. When we skedaddled out of here, we'd head south away from the peaks, but it was nice to know there was another way out, in case Murphy showed his ugly head. The next move was to find a decent observation post to watch the comings and goings, which had to be where I couldn't be seen or stepped on by accident, and could be easily vacated.

While I was crawling around, I found a likely spot not too far from where the dumb-assed Indian almost ran into the fence. I rigged up some security around my newfound observation post and named it Custer's Last Stand.

After I finished rigging up the OP, there was time to settle in and do some serious observation of the compound. With the scope from my rifle I spotted the truck spewing the diesel smoke I'd seen earlier. It was sitting in front of the largest building in the compound yard, and several men were off loading large boxes from it. The uniforms worn by the little fuckers were regular NVA, but the truck was an old American GI six-by. There were six uniforms, including the driver and the guy riding shotgun. I was wondering how they had acquired the old truck; it looked to be from the forties. How many more troops were in the compound also came to mind.

The largest of the buildings looked like a huge barracks, with double doors on both ends and blacked-out windows down each side. There were four smaller buildings, built by the Dutch or French, that looked to be about two feet off the ground.

For five hours I observed the compound, then for safety's sake I crawled around the whole facility once again. I couldn't believe they had zero security, zippo, nada, none. No guards, no towers or shacks. Score one for the home team, the white hats.

When I crawled back to the OP, the activity inside the fence began to pick up as four very large figures walked towards the big building in the middle. These guys were too big for VC or NVA. After watching them for a while, it hit me—they were POWs! Their clothing was tattered and worn but clean. Thin would be a good way to describe their condition, but not bad considering their plight. I wondered how many POWs there were, because that could present additional problems. If there were more, I hoped they were in the same, if not better, condition than the four coming across the yard.

As I digested the unexpected turn of events, I saw something that made my heart skip a beat. Just coming into view behind the POWs was an additional group of tall people: two men and a blonde woman, all in civilian cloths. BINGO! I knew Primrose would be happier than shit to hear about the big blonde. Wow, what luck, the Gods must be looking out for us! The blonde sure looked funny in the mix of POWs and NVA, carrying herself well, head up and proud. I bet they had one hell of a time getting her to do anything she didn't want to. With her stature, all she'd have to do is look down on one of those pukes, and they would be intimidated—good for her!

They were all headed for one of the smaller buildings; by the smell in the air, it was chow time. The walk was short, and they all seemed to be in good physical condition, which was good news. Had there been someone on crutches or—worse yet—a stretcher case, it would have presented major escape problems.

Chow lasted about forty minutes. After leaving the chow hall, the trio was escorted over to the large building. "Chaperones" would be a better term for their guards, never coming close to them, keeping a good distance. The POWs were also loosely guarded as they wandered around picking up trash.

Sometime after the trio entered the big building, there was the sound of music, which lasted about an hour. The sounds meant they were in rehearsal, which would lend one to think they were going to perform somewhere and not heading for the dungeon or firing squad. When the sounds ceased, the trio was again loosely escorted to a smaller building, which appeared to be their confinement quarters. If things went right, their next escort would be US Marines, and their next performance in Saigon or Hong Kong.

The light was starting to ebb a little, and everyone disappeared, no traffic, dead silence. With the sudden lack of activity, it might be that a satellite came over this time every day. All their precautions were for naught, because I knew where they were and so did the brass—the clock was ticking on this facility. The camp was totally blacked out and so quiet you could hear a pin drop, with only occasional light leaking from a cracked door.

While watching the dark outline of the buildings, it occurred to me they must have tunnels to go from one building to another and probably some escape tunnels that would go beyond the fence line. I would need to do my Indian shit again tomorrow and look for possible existence of tunnels that could be used by our team as well as theirs. I hated this daylight work; it screwed up my night vision, and then I couldn't see shit at night. It was time to sack out. Now I lay me down to sleep, let the shamans count the sheep and show me visions I can keep.

When the breaking dawn somewhere above the canopy started to peek through the foliage, I began my search for the tunnels I believed were there. I hoped they had thought more about their escape than they had about security—we could use the tunnels.

If there were tunnels there, we would need to control them from the get-go.

I crawled around the fence line again, and then again with the same results as the first time: nothing. So I started around again and, with all the skill of a seasoned tracker, I fell into a large hole I had missed on three occasions. How the hell had I missed something so big? Brushing myself off, I looked up, and there was a tunnel heading right for the compound. This had to be an escape tunnel from the compound, and it was six feet in height, with room for three abreast. I headed up the tunnel to be sure, but didn't go too far, not wanting to reveal my discovery by accidentally running into one of those NVA fuckers and having to kill him: that would leave loose ends. Backing out of the tunnel, I put everything back in its place, to cover my tracks. Indians know how to do such things. According to white-eyes legend Indians leave no tracks, white eyes leave heap big mess.

I crawled back to the OP and settled in once again to observe the compound. The POWs were out cleaning the area again. For some reason they never looked up and it was impossible to see their faces, but there was something about a couple of them that was making my skin quiver. I whispered to myself, "I would dearly love to set you guys free. Hang on—the cavalry is on the way."

After three days of observing the compound, I discovered their routine was consistent. It was time to head back to the LZ and a nice chopper ride home. Thoughts of being followed never came up, because the bad guys never knew I had visited them. It'd be a pleasure to lead the troops back here and liberate the camp.

I followed the trail marks I had left on the way in and had no trouble finding the LZ for pickup. The area was as quiet as I left it. For sure the next trip down the trail wouldn't be.

Just before dark I could hear the sweet sound of the Huey rotor blades, so I put out a little smoke, and the chopper found me right on target and on time. With little ado the bird hovered over me, and down came the lifeline. With some assistance, I clambered through the hatch for the ride back.

I still didn't feel good about flying; Indians were supposed to soar like eagles, which meant I had a defective gene from somewhere in the past. Putting on the headset was no easy task, but when I had it on, the captain asked me, "How was your vacation in Laos?"

Talking over the roar of the engines was no small feat, even with the headset. I told Captain Schroud the mission had been fruitful and Primrose would have to fill him in on the details. With that, I kicked back and tried to get in tune with the engines and rotor noise. The country from the air was a different world than on the ground, and it was remarkable how beautiful it was. Too bad it had such a hostile environment in the jungles and meadows, but one of these days the violence would end, and the bad guys would go back up north where they belonged and the people could get back to their lives.

I couldn't wait to report my findings to Primrose. He'd be ecstatic about Rhonda and her dad and it'd be nice for a change to report something good, in this backwater armpit of the earth.

CHAPTER 13

In the Compound

"Well, what do you think, Jack?"

"I don't know, Fred, if they're trying to find us now or not—if they ever were. I guess they would have made some kind of rescue effort, if only to look like they were, and I bet it would be some half-assed effort, thinking we were already tits up. Not being officially with the USO, we really had no standing, and when they found the bodies of our security guards, they surely weren't too optimistic about our health."

"Listen, dad, let's not lose hope on this. You guys have been in tight spots before, and they haven't treated us badly so far. I believe Zach is out there pulling every string and pushing every button to rescue us."

"Rhonda, I think Jack and I would be at the top of Zach's hit list for letting us talk him into agreeing for you to come on this gig. He'll probably finish what the NVA has started!"

"Don't blame yourselves, guys. If the truck hadn't broken down, we wouldn't be here. Ours was an abduction of opportunity, and don't forget Zach's out there somewhere."

"Rhonda, because I'm the leader of the world famous Jack Mont Trio, I have a few words of wisdom from past experience. As long as we're entertaining these little shits, we have a chance for rescue, but once they tire of us, they'll kill Fred and me, and you'll be sold to the highest bidder. You might want to think of an easier way out. What would be in store for you would be horrible at best."

"Okay, Jack, Rhonda—enough of that shit, let's get back to reality. It's time for chow. Let's get over to the slop-chute, and we can talk to the POWs, who've been confined for years. They were a happy group when we arrived, thinking someone would be hot on our trail for rescue. What a letdown that must have been for them to know the cavalry wasn't on our heels. But they've been a great help since we arrived."

"Just think, Rhonda, your dad and I went through WWII without a scratch, and now look what's happened. All we wanted was to play a little music, get paid a decent wage, and travel. Shit, let's go to chow."

#

"Rhonda what did the big POW guy say to you as we walked to chow?"

"Dad, he said, 'Rhonda just keep walking so we can talk, the little VC assholes like to poke the big POWs in the back every chance they get. How are things going for you guys?' I told him we were fine, but you and Jack were getting a little spooked because no attempts have been made to rescue us.

" 'No big deal, Rhonda,' he told me. We've been at it for years. You're always looking over your shoulder hoping the Marines will show up and save the day. You have to get used to conditions and live one day at a time and be happy you're still alive and in good shape. In your case—great shape. I don't want to get your hopes up, but a couple of times today the hair stood up on my neck, and it only does that when something I can't see is happening or about to happen. There were no little VC or NVA jerks around, so that something came from outside the compound. It may not mean anything, but my instincts are usually very good. Stay tuned for hair-raising bulletins. I'll talk to you again after chow. Don't give up the ship, a rescue may not only originate from the outside!"

"Rhonda, did he have anything to say about where they were from or how long they've been held captive?"

"No, just what I said. I'm curious about one thing, though. Why haven't they told us their names?"

"Rhonda, the big guy told Jack the less we knew about them the better off we were. No use getting punished for something on their account."

CHAPTER 14

Scout Sniper Company Area

"Holy shit, Toms, they're alive, and you observed them in the compound! No mistakes on this one, right?"

"Yes, Primrose, not only the trio, but there are also four POWs with them."

"What kind of condition were they in?"

"Primrose, I saw seven captives in excellent condition, taking into consideration the ordeal they've been through. The trio practices music in the morning and plays for the troops at night. The POWs are the camp labor force, cleaning and general ground maintenance. The LRRP guy was right on with the coordinates, and the compound is about three hours by foot from the LZ on the border, maybe less now that there's a marked trail."

"Damn, Toms, do you realize how close that is to the border?"

"Zach, the jungle is really thick there, and the canopy is so low, the place looks like a ghost in the mist."

While Toms was giving me a detailed account of his mission, I was in outer space thinking about Rhonda. The urgency I felt had just tripled. Toms also told me there was something about the POWs that made the hair on his neck stand at attention. He couldn't put his finger on it, but it was there in spades.

"Toms, it's time to see Captain Easy and lay out all we have so far and devise a plan of attack."

"What's this we shit, Kemosabe? You present it to him."

"Okay, Chicken Little."

"Wait, Zach—before you go see Easy, I almost forgot, Captain Schroud wants to meet with you ASAP about something life threatening. You might want to wait on Easy until you talk to him. He was really excited about whatever it was he wanted to tell you."

"Okay Toms, I'll wait until tomorrow afternoon to see Captain Easy. I'll see Schroud in the morning while he's on his milk run and robbing someone. You get some sleep. I'll come by after dark tomorrow, and we can go into more detail about your mission."

"Primrose, don't forget I have a mission here besides yours, so let's make the meeting short. I need to go hunting."

#

I met with Schroud the next morning, while he was in the process of trading two jeeps and a six-by in return for a year's supply of scotch, six months' worth of gin, a chit for a couple of hundred steaks to be picked up as needed, and four boxes of penicillin.

"Where did you get the vehicles, Captain?"

"They came from the Seabees camp."

"Did you trade for them or steal them?"

"It's not stealing, Zach, it's just moving government property from one location to another without all the red tape—a typical government operation that is not recorded."

"So what did you give for the vehicles?"

"I gave the Seabees a Manitowoc crane I had shipped over from Okinawa. Don't ask any more questions Primrose. If I told you everything I knew, it would put me out of business. Besides all this bullshit, I have something very important to tell you, so shut up a minute and listen!"

"Jesus, lighten up, Dave."

"Listen, Primrose, Toms filled me in on finding the camp, the trio, and the POWs. Finding Rhonda and her dad was great news, but there is some bad news I have to report. The reason they weren't looking for the trio is because they have known about the camp, the trio, and the POWs all along. The G-2 section had a snitch in the camp, and if there was a rescue attempt the intelligence would terminate. It's their opinion that anyone that would cause the Intel to stop would be expendable. But all that has changed, because the informant was transferred a couple of weeks ago.

"According to their last intel, there is a big conference planned there for next week, with top guns from the NVA and VC attending. The meeting will be seven days from today, and division intends to vaporize the camp, no matter who's there. You have until next Friday to get your people out!"

"How the hell did you come by this information?"

"You know, Zach, you ask too many questions. I can't tell you my sources. Take the info for what it is, and act on it—the information is accurate. I'm telling you they are going to level the compound, and whoever is there will be toast. A rescue by division is out, because they don't want to tip their hand. It's up to you and any more crazy fuckers you can get to help you. Your odds for success wouldn't even be posted in a Vegas casino sports book."

I told the captain I had a plan that might get Rhonda and the rest out and into Thailand before anyone knew what happened. I thought if we played our cards right, we could pull it off.

"You know, Captain Schroud, we'll have to take everyone out."

"Sure, I know that. We will."

I was thinking if we did this right, division wouldn't be able to do squat—if they even found out about it. They wouldn't try to court-martial us, because then the whole affair would come out, and the press would eat them alive for risking innocent civilians and our own POWs, all for the sake of getting a few high-ranking VC and NVA officers.

"So are you in, Captain?"

"Shit, Primrose, how many times do I have to tell you? My middle name is Adventure. Hell yes, I'm in!"

"Thanks, Captain, I'll get back to you after I meet with Easy."

"Oh, by the way, Primrose, all the news isn't bad. I have two gunship crews who are adventurers and crazy that would like to give you a hand. They have their choppers deadlined up north for a week, and they'll put some kick behind your ass if you need it. Friday is the last day they can help, don't let it slip away."

Without another word, Schroud jumped into his Huey, lifted off, and wagging his tail, headed south. I suppose all pilots live their lives close to the edge, fancying themselves adventure specialists.

From the tarmac I headed back to the company area, looking for Toms. I found him asleep, his face covered with a black mask. I gently awakened him, ducking a right hand, and when he was fully awake, I told him what Schroud said about the camp being targeted.

Toms went into orbit about the new information. "Those fucking, lying-ass, white-eyed sons-a-bitches would kill their own people and call it collateral damage. Fuck-em, we'll liberate the camp on our own."

"Toms, with this new information, is there anything more you need to do?"

"Look, with only a few days to get the mission on track, a return to the compound is imperative, Primrose. I'll retrace my steps from the LZ to the camp and then take another look at the tunnel, talk to the POWs, and in general dissect the whole area again."

"I may be able to help you with the tunnel search. I know a tracker from Okinawa who is the best there is when it comes to jungle shit. He offered his services when I first arrived at Camp Schwab, and the military brass, along with the black ops guys shortchanged him, so he would like to embarrass them any way he can. I can get him. Anything else?"

"Yes. We need an explosives expert to blow the compound and implode the tunnels once we are out of range. It would be an insurance package, just in case the fast movers fuck up and miss."

"I'll find a powder monkey who is crazy enough to go with us. While I'm thinking of it, how was the LZ you picked out?"

"Well, I didn't pick it out—Schroud did, and it wasn't good. I had to rope down. We'll be in a hurry coming out and won't have time to be climbing any rope ladders. It would be nice to have enough room to set two choppers down."

"Don't think that'll be a problem. Our high explosives guy can blow us an LZ. See you tonight Toms; good hunting."

"You know, Zach, if you would quit bothering me, I could get some shut-eye and be bright-eyed and bushy-tailed tonight. You want to come along?"

"No thanks, Toms."

After leaving Toms, I headed over to the Scout Sniper Platoon area looking for J. T. Martin, who was due back from the bush. He'd been pulling duty with a grunt company that had a VC sniper giving them fits. Martin had gone up to take him out, and from the news I'd heard, he had done just that. I found him at the rifle range. He was not one to rest on yesterday's achievements.

"Well, if it isn't Corporal Primrose, the man on a mission! Where are you with the rescue attempt?"

I replied that it was coming together and brought him up to date. He was happy about my family and concerned that if anything went wrong on the rescue attempt, the fast movers sent by division would certainly finish things.

I explained about the tunnels Toms found and wondered if he knew an explosives expert, someone in Combat Engineers, because we wanted to level the whole compound and implode the tunnels on the way out.

"Primrose, I do know a guy who is just that, a powder monkey first class, who's been bunking here. But there's a small problem: he's in the brig, and he's crazier than that fucking Indian you have on your payroll."

"What's he in the brig for?"

"Primrose, don't you think too many people are getting in on this capricious little caper? One leak is bound to find Murphy all over your ass!"

"I agree, but things have to be done, and we've only six days to get the mission on track and in motion. New tell me about the combat engineer."

"The guy's name is T. C. Champion, and he's from Wyoming. I don't know what the T. C. stands for, but his nickname is Two Case. He can literally drink two cases of beer before going into the ville to party. His present home in the brig is for something you may not believe—you may want to just leave his ass there. That crazy son of a bitch blew the three top floors off a Saigon whorehouse because one of the bitches there took his money and went downstairs to get change and never came back. So he goes looking for her to get his money, and then the mama san gets in the middle of things, so the shit hit the fan. She goes bananas, calls the military police. He gets away before the MPs arrive, but not for long. Later that night he comes back with a Colt .45 auto and a satchel full of high explosives. He gets everyone out of the whorehouse by yelling fire.

"When everyone is out, he rigs the top three floors with C-4 or whatever it was he had in the bag. He then announces he'll blow the place if he doesn't get his money back or get laid. Everyone is too scared to answer, so just before the MPs and fire department show up, he pulls the trigger on the HE. You guessed it, the top three floors disappear, and nothing else is damaged. Champion is out in front when it goes, laughing like a madman, yelling how beautiful it is. Now there's a man who enjoys his work. Champion's talent is being wasted. When he's not in the brig, he's a file clerk."

"Yes, Martin, I know all about the office-pinky shit."

"So the MPs pick him up, and he's now waiting on the investigation to be completed to see what they'll do to him. Chances are they'll try and pay off the mama san and transfer Champion to Alaska or somewhere just as far away; that way the lid stays on the whole business. "One thing for sure, Champion didn't get laid and never got his money back, although he may have gotten off when he pulled the plug on the upper three floors of the cathouse."

"I'd like to talk to the crazy fucker, sounds like our kind of guy!"

"Sure, we can visit him no sweat. The visiting hours are irregular, so anytime you want we can go."

"Martin, why was Champion bunking in the scout sniper area?"

"In its wisdom the Corps decided to put all the whackos in one place. Division thinks scout snipers are all crazy anyway, so our area is a good place for the misfits until their particular talent is needed. Nobody fucks around in our area, and there's always a need for crazies like us. You and Champion are perfect examples."

"How about we go see him right now!"

"Sure, let's go."

Martin and I walked over to the brig, which was a broken-down old hotel that had been reinforced, but if anyone really wanted they could just go headfirst through the walls. The turnkey gave us thirty minutes with Champion, who was all starched and squared away—not bad for a crazy fucker.

Martin introduced us and asked if he would like to get out of his present surroundings.

"Hell yes, Martin, you think I like it here? How would you get me out of here, anyway? They caught me red-handed, no doubt about who blew the building up—if you could call that dump a building. I could have shoved it over, kinda like this one here. That building wasn't much of a challenge for a guy with my talent. Sure was fun, though."

"Corporal Primrose has some favors due in high places and might be willing to use them in your behalf."

"Champion, I can call in a couple of those IOUs and you're out of here, but there are strings attached. If you agree to go on a special mission, you'll be able to use your God-given talents to blow things up, lots of things."

"Primrose, any mission which allows me to blow things up, I'm interested in—count me in. The chow here sucks, the other fuckers in here are crazy, and the racks are lumpy. It's hell being the only dude in here of sound mind and body. I have no one to talk to. If you guys get me out of here, I'll owe you for life, no matter the outcome. Don't be long though, because this place may be a distant memory before long.

I've discovered a way to level this joint and disappear into the bush, never to be seen again."

We used our allotted thirty minutes before the turnkey took Champion back to his cell.

I said to Martin on the way out, "Champion doesn't seem to be short any bricks."

"No, Zach, he has a good background, with education from the University of Wyoming, football player and baseball all star, etc. The family has a demolition business, and if he were at home he wouldn't be considered crazy, but going overboard here is easy in this free-for-all world we work in. Do it to them before they do it to you, so to speak."

"Thanks for the help, Martin. I now have three recruits: a crazy Indian, one pissed-off Okinawan, and a whacko powder monkey—some crew, huh?"

Martin retorted, "Don't forget me, asshole; I'm in on this war party too! You think I'm going through all this trouble just for old times' sake?"

I told Martin it was time to bring the latest news up to Captain Easy. He should be on his third martini by now. Later, I would get Captain Schroud to find a case of gin for Easy, to keep him in a perpetual good mood.

We found Captain Easy in his tent as expected, but he didn't want to talk there, so we all walked over to Martin's tent for the conference, where I laid out what we knew and the progress of putting a team together.

"Primrose."

"Yes sir."

"You're as crazy as those dipshits who have thrown in with you. Now let's be realistic. It's almost impossible to get this going in six days. We may not be talking D-day here, but it still requires days of planning. You know this is my third martini, and my head is a little soft. You tell me how to do the impossible, Zach!"

"Yes sir, that's what Marines do sir—the impossible. For starters, Toms needs to go back for another look and wants the tracker and a powder monkey to go with him. Champion, the guy in the brig, is our HE expert, if you can spring him. Schroud has his ship and two gunships on deadline waiting for our call. What we need from Marine Air are two choppers to lift our asses out of the LZ. Our needs from supply are covered, no questions asked. We'll be in and out about the time division sends in the fast movers to dump on the place, and we may have a little surprise for them."

"You didn't tell me about division!"

"It just came up, sir."

"That's the reason for the six-day deadline?"

"Yes sir."

"Let's wait for Tom's final recon, then bring me your plans for liberation, and I'll make my evaluation at that time for a go or no-go. For now I need to work on Champion's confinement, which will require me to use his mental status as a ruse. The hospital ship on Yankee Station would be a good place to hide him for a couple of weeks, but not send him right away. The medical officer is fond of martinis and he's over at the O Club as we speak. Get to work, gentlemen."

The following day the captain got Champion out and had him confined to the Scout Sniper area to be ready for the mission. He told the doc he would keep him in the area until his appointment on the ship. The turnkey had his suspicions, but he didn't give a shit about what was going on, because he was a short-timer.

"Primrose, when is the tracker coming aboard?"

"Sir, Heto will be here in the morning. Martin and I will meet him. Heto has some flyboys over on the Rock that owe him big time. He wouldn't go into details, but he has them by the short hairs. . . . Sir."

"What now Primrose? Jesus—does it never end!"

"Captain Schroud called; he'll pick up Toms and crew in the morning. Martin and I will see they get mounted up and on their way."

The beautiful sound of the Huey was music to the ears, as it dropped down to the tarmac right on time. Martin and I loaded T. C., Toms, and the tracker Heto aboard. I yelled "Tangerine," code name for the mission. Thumbs up was their return gesture, and away they went in another cloud of red dust. Toms picked the code; Indians like bright colors, and he's especially fond of red—blood red. The chopper was up, up, and away, and it reminded me of the Lone Ranger leaving town on his white stallion, only this time the mount was yellow and black. The updated First Cav's horse patrol would drop the three rogues at Toms's new LZ.

CHAPTER 15

Laos

I was thinking, What is my Indian ass doing with all this white man's shit? That Primrose has gotten me into something other than my stated goal of getting even for my brothers. If this doesn't work out, I'll scalp the SOB in the English tradition.

"Champion, can you make this LZ big enough for two choppers?"

"Sure, no problem Toms; with the right stuff, I could make it big enough for a C-130 to set down. Could be we might need a little of Puff the Magic Dragon before we get out of here. This is really cool; if I can do a few jobs like this one, I'm going to have one hell of a good time on this sortie."

Grinning from ear to ear, Champion had that look of a guy who just put one over on his high school principal. He was definitely in hog heaven.

Heto the tracker started yelling for us to get moving. "We're burning daylight, it's already close to dark under the jungle canopy."

We headed away from the LZ into the dense jungle, Heto leading the way. Heto wanted to backtrack the trail I left coming out. After about twenty minutes on the trail, Heto announced, "American Indian leave trail a blind man could follow."

"No shit, Heto, me American Indian, leave heap big trail, because we won't have time for compass classes on the way out."

"If Indian was so good at being quiet, there shouldn't be anyone on his trail!"

"There was no one to hear me, because their security is nonexistent, but we still need to cover all our bases. When we reach the OP, you'll see what I mean."

The hump wasn't so bad the second time around. Heto and T. C. thought I was some kind of pussy, the way I complained about how thick the jungle was. We were about two hours plus, when Heto stumbled into the OP, just about like I did the first time. I didn't give him any shit about almost running into the fence, but his expression told me he wasn't pleased with the little smile that crossed my face.

There was some daylight left and Heto wanted to take a good look at the tunnel, so I showed him the tunnel entrance. While he was taking a look, T. C. and I set up our defense and got serious about observing the compound.

While T. C. and I had the compound under surveillance, Heto came crawling up and said, "There are many tunnels like this one all over Vietnam, Laos, and Cambodia; they aren't hard to find."

"Look man, they can't be that easy to find—I didn't find them!"

"You're not Okinawan jungle tracker guy like me. You stick to Indian shit, and let me take care of gook shit."

With that he displayed a big smile and evaporated into the jungle. So T. C. and I began our vigil on the compound once again. I noticed there was a lot more activity than before, with lots of brass running around.

While watching the compound, I asked T. C. how he became an expert with explosives.

"Before I tell you my life's story, Toms, I would like to thank you getting me out of the brig. Maybe if we do some good here, higher authority will let me off the hook for the cathouse thing."

"T. C., I hate to be the bearer of bad news, but if division ever finds out what we're up to here, we'll be in Leavenworth, not in the local brig. Besides I didn't spring you from the brig. Cpl. Primrose and Capt. Easy had you released. They think you are as crazy as I am, so let's take it one day at a time."

"Listen, Toms, if you want to know how I became a powder monkey, here's how it went. My family came over from Eastern Europe; they were all miners, who settled in Wyoming because of the mining and the climate. When the underground mines played out, the open-pit mines opened. We adjusted and then came work with the highway department. Over the years we have stayed in the pyrotechnic end of things, and I've followed in the footsteps of my father and grandfather. I may be the best of the lot. I'm very good at blowing things up, down, out, in, or any way you want it. What we have here is an art form, learned over many years.

"When I finish my enlistment, I'm going into the demolition business. And for me being crazy: maybe a little. I like the handle, it keeps people away from me. It helps to be a little off, to handle the high explosives that I do. If you pucker easy you're in the wrong business."

"I think you're crazy, T. C.'"

"You notice they always come around looking for us crazy fuckers when something needs doing and they don't have the balls for it. So here we are, the hidden assets no one talks about."

As darkness began setting in like a San Francisco fog, I watched the compound and T. C. slept. With my attention focused on the buildings,

I caught this movement in the comer of my eye, and coming out of the mist like a ghost was Heto. I wondered how he did that appearing and disappearing shit all the time. He just appeared and disappeared at will.

Walking up to the OP, Heto said to me, "I've found two more tunnels you overlooked. A sightless old woman could have found them. Some Indian tracker you are! I'll find more; the bad guys will have plenty of escape routes. And we should check out this tunnel, all the way to the end."

I woke up T. C., who would need to survey the tunnels to determine the amount of HE he would need to implode them. Heading down the tunnel, I was in the lead, followed by Heto and then Champion, who wanted to assess all the tunnels, regardless of whether they were constructed the same or not.

At the end of the tunnel there was an old wooden ladder that stood almost straight up, the last rung just below a metal hatch. Being in the lead, I climbed the ladder and pushed the hatch up very slowly, hoping no one was waiting to put a bullet in my head. The hatch opened right between the mess hall and the prisoners' barracks. Holding the heavy door open, I couldn't see anyone near or far. The gods must be on our side on this one. It was perfect: we'd waylay the guards, drop everybody down the hatch, and head for freedom—piece of cake! By the time anyone got suspicious we'd be long gone, and Champion would have it ready to implode. Not long after our little tunnel adventure, the fast movers would arrive with their air strike from division. Our vote was no B-52s; we might not be far enough way.

I slid the cover back over the opening and climbed back down the ladder just as Champion had caught up with us, saying, "The tunnel won't be a problem to bring in, it's just hard dirt, with no shoring. Are we gonna contact anyone inside?"

"No, Champion. Primrose thinks we should hold off as long as possible before getting anyone inside involved, because we want them to act naturally. It would be a disaster if one of them overacted and piqued some unwanted attention from the guards."

#

Backtracking down the tunnel to the OP, T. C. was explaining how he was going to set his HE and what the results would be. It was a lesson from a sick mind.

I said to Heto, "When we get back to the OP and settled in, I want you to tell me how you got a Navy jet to bring you to Da Nang from Okinawa, without so much as a how do you do from anyone.'"

After retreating back to the OP and setting a defense for the night, Heto agreed to fill me in on his power over the Armed Forces of the United States, Far East Command.

"I speak several languages, including Japanese, Russian, Chinese, Vietnamese, and of course English. That puts me in the catbird seat with the black ops world. They had a mole in place, way up north near the Chinese border, and I was hired to snatch this guy and bring him south. Being a good trader, I agreed to for x-amount of dollars and some unlimited favors of all sorts. My demands were taken with a grain of salt, but they had little choice and agreed to my terms.

"I never did see any money, but I'm having fun with the favors part, with a letter that has all the right signatures and stamps on it—I get what I want. The mission to chaperone the guy I was supposed to snatch started off with a parachute drop fifty miles off course, so after some serious humping I finally found the right village, and it didn't take long to find the mole. He was not pleased about a trip south, but under the circumstances, he had little choice in the matter. I headed south with him in tow, sniveling every step of the way. I personally didn't think the little fuck was worth the trouble.

"When we were about half way, the prick decided to bail on me, because he was sure his paymaster wanted him dead. It took me two days to track the shitbird down, and by then I was tempted to kill the puke myself, but then I would have to tell the black ops guys he got himself killed on the way down. I figured they wouldn't live up to their end of the bargain if I didn't have proof of his demise, and I would have to carry his dead ass the rest of the way to show them, so I let him live. I told him if they wanted him dead, I would've killed his dumb ass already.

"I found out later he was a high muckamuck in the Communist Party. The Commies were going to kill him for treason, for they had suspicions of his mole status. The poor guy didn't know who to trust; if I hadn't gotten him out when I did, he would now be a member of the dearly departed.

"It wasn't long after our return that he was found dead. The story going around was that the black ops guys did a number on him and made it look like suicide. Makes you wonder who are the good guys! So they owe me big time, and every now and then I collect. They're way behind on their payments. So there it is, good night."

As daylight came filtering through the canopy, it made me think, Wow, this place is really beautiful and peaceful! But then the senses kick in for a rude awakening. The senses tell you this is a battlefield with a free-fire zone. You are either alert or dead, no in-the-middle shit! It was time to get the day started with cold chow and no smoking. I sent Heto to search for more tunnels and T. C. Champion to trek through all the tunnels discovered so far, to estimate the HE needs. My job was to monitor the compound and take notice of any patterns by the enemy and the good guys. Timing would be critical for the rescue to have any chance of success. There were still no guards except for the few walking with the POWs and civilians, which was not the best way to run a railroad.

The camp was starting to fill up with lots of field grade officers, so the information from division was accurate. Score another one for the good guys. We'd have to assume the bad guys had beefed up their security and cover accordingly.

The trio of POWs showed up right on time, heading for the chow hall. If they could hang in there for a couple more days, they'd be in for the surprise of their lives.

Damn, those POWs set off all kinds of alarms and made the hair on my neck stand on end. I wished one of them would raise his head just a little so I could get a good look at his face. I needed to put my finger on what the hell was bugging me about them. A face-to-face meeting was definitely in the picture.

While I was watching the compound, I saw something out of the comer of my eye again, and it startled me, thinking they might have beefed up security and I hadn't see it coming. As I was getting ready to take on whoever it was that caught my eye, Heto jumped into the OP from the other side with his knife drawn, ready to cut my throat. "You know, Toms, you are supposed to be a great Indian tracker, hunter, and warrior. Shit, I could have done you in just now! Were all the movies I saw about the West bullshit or what?"

"Jesus, Heto, you scared the shit out of me. You have to stop this appearing out of nowhere crap. You've taken five years off me the last two times you've done that shit. Before I was rudely interrupted, I was watching some movement; I think we have company."

"I know, Indian scout, I just saved your red ass from sure death. I'm the king of jungle trackers, so let's see what it was you saw."

While we headed over to the area where I had seen the movement, Heto never stopped telling me how great he was.

"Do you see those tracks, Toms?"

"Sure—so what?"

"Those are tiger tracks, and I just saved you dumb ass from being eaten by a very big pussy cat. You now owe me big time!"

"I'm sure I'll have plenty of opportunity for payback during this mission—let's get back to business. Okay, Heto, tell me about the tunnels."

"There are six tunnels in all, and the one here, I recommend for our rescue. The others are about the same size, but we're lucky to have this one at our disposal."

"Look, Heto, here comes Champion! Damn, he could use some recon training; he sounds like a freight train coming through a tunnel. Maybe you could teach him some of the disappearing shit you do!"

"Hello, fellow team members, your resident explosives expert has returned."

"So what do you think of the tunnels Heto has found, T. C.?"

"It's a piece of cake, Toms. With the right stuff I can close all the tunnels on our way out, no sweat. The buildings are a different breed; I need a closer look at them. I think the buildings are about two feet off the ground, which is good for us. They look like wood, but I need to know what's underneath with a hands-on inspection, roam over them, feel them."

"Shit, Champion, we're not talking about a woman here!"

"Okay, okay, it just feels so good to know I'm gonna make sawdust out of them."

#

After observing the camp all day, I decided to make an attempt to talk with the POWs and get some inside help, along with finding out what was bugging me about them. I told T. C. we'd head down the tunnel that night and get with the POWs. He thought that was a good idea, but I had to remind him, "T. C., you have to remember, you are not slick like Heto the tracker or me the great Indian scout. You have to be very careful, and not sound like a freight train. Okay?"

"You know, Toms, I may not be a slick Indian or tracker, but I bet I can be nimble around some very high explosives that would make your red skin turn pale yellow. I can be as cool as anyone when the cake is in the oven."

"Heto, you stay here and keep a sharp eye out; they may increase the security with all the field grade officers around. They can't continue to be so lax. This place hasn't had any trouble in the past, and that's going to change, big time, but we can't be too careful. One of those dumb asses may just stumble upon us, like I did the tunnel entrance, which means we'd have to kill the fucker and hope he wasn't missed. We can't raise any flags and screw up our rescue or division's air power demonstration. If we do this right, no one will know we've been here until the sound of the HE is heard. The password for tonight is *hocus-pocus.* If you hear a lot of noise coming down the tunnel later, lock and load—you'll know the powder monkey fucked up, and the Indian is saving his white ass."

When T. C. and I reached the ladder and were about to start up, we both stopped at the same time, because dirt was falling from the hole cover. Someone was pulling the cover to one side, which meant we'd have to kill whoever it was and hope he wasn't missed for awhile. Shit!

I pushed T. C. aside and climbed up the ladder as fast as I could, so I could be there when the cover came off. The cover was being pushed aside very slowly—too slowly. It was like someone was waiting for the jack-in-the-box to explode. Just as the cover exposed an arm, I grabbed it and jerked the body down through the opening, both of us falling headfirst down to the tunnel floor. Champion grabbed the intruder and was about to slit his throat, when we heard the sounds of some very choice American four-letter words. Champion just held him while I ran up the ladder and closed the opening. While I was pulling the cover shut, the hair stood up on my neck again, big time!

I slid down the ladder quickly. Champion turned on his flashlight, and when my feet hit the deck, he had the light on our guest.

With the light shining on his face, I just stood there like a cigar store Indian, my mouth hanging open like the mouth of the Missouri River. T. C. released our uninvited guest and when he stood up, he was just about as tall as me, and I was looking into the eyes of another Indian. Staring back at me were the eyes and big smile of my dead brother. Jesus! While I stood there staring like a complete idiot, the other Indian started talking.

"We knew you were coming, we felt the vibes for days. The feelings began when the musical group arrived, and we knew then help was on the way and who it would be. The shamans have given us clear dreams. Well, say something, little brother!"

The guy with the big grin on his kisser was my brother, Rick D. Toms. I was speechless for the first time in my life; my mouth wouldn't engage. I just stared at what the beam of light was showing me. He was supposed to be dead, going on six years. When I finally found my vocal cords, I managed to say something real stupid.

"You look pretty good in this dim light, for a dead Indian. Where's Dick?"

"Dick's in the barracks, watching out for our guard. I'm scouting the tunnels for our way out of this pigsty. With all the officers running around here, we thought it might be a good time for the good guys to do a hit on this dump. Dick and I figured it was about time to head out of here and take our chances in the jungle. When the vibes started coming, and we knew help was on the way, our next move was to be sure about the best way to leave the premises. How the hell did you find this place?"

"Rick, we don't have time for all the details right now. My friend Champion here, who was about to cut your red-ass throat, is an explosives expert, and he needs a hands-on look at all the buildings here. Our plan is to vaporize this rotten apple when you two ugly Indians and the others are heading down the tunnel to freedom's door. You were right when you said the good guys would dump on this place sooner or later. Well, it's sooner—like Friday is D-Day. We need to be out of here by 1800 on dump day. Can you take my friend around to all the buildings without being seen?"

"No problem, little brother. We go out every night for a little rock and roll, when the musicians do their show. Dick and I have buried seven of these little fuckers, and they aren't missed, because the officers think they have deserted or have been eaten by tigers, so they don't bother to look for them."

"Please don't mention tigers!"

Rick looked at me with moist eyes and gave me a big bear hug. Then he and T. C. Champion disappeared up the ladder and into the night. Damn, everybody seems to disappear better than I do, and I'm the expert. I wondered if Rick and Dick had thought about how much back pay they had coming or how they would spend it. I also wondered how they were still alive, if there was an eyewitness to their demise. How did the witness get it so wrong? Another question came to mind, about how a mother of three Indian boys was going to handle the news that two of the boys who were supposed to be in the happy hunting grounds were in fact alive and well? If the rescue went as planned, three alive and well boys would be going home, with no body bags this time around.

The shamans needed to conjure up some good juju and send us on our way intact and whole. Suddenly I realized I was now back to third in succession to be chief. Five minutes earlier, I had been number one. Maybe I should leave one and two here! No, couldn't do that, they would just show up later and be the heroes they are. No matter what, I'm going to change my name to Tom E. Fingers, and after I get my law degree, I'll run for reservation chief of police. At least that moniker has *chief* in the title. And then I'll run for judge.

I directed my mind back into the bush; mistakes come easy when your head isn't in the present. Good Indian tracker doesn't make mistakes.

Boy, would Primrose be surprised about the turn of events, and that we'd have help from inside. The need for more weapons and ammo would be high on the agenda. We might need the extra firepower to get the hell out of Dodge. With Champion doing his thing, we'd leave a serious message: Don't fuck with the Indians, it's not healthy!

Damn, I wished those two would get back. They'd been gone a long time. But maybe I was being a little impatient. It's not every day that two dead brothers come back to life after six years. I was about to climb up the ladder for a look, when the tunnel door slid aside and down came T. C. with Rick right on his ass. They were both laughing so hard they couldn't talk.

"What the hell is so funny?"

T. C. said, "Rick and I were looking at the building which houses the mess hall, the one closest to the tunnel here, and there was a cook standing on the porch smoking. Rick says, 'Watch this,' and put one of the electrical wires running alongside and under the building next to the porch. This dumb-fuck cook whips out his unit and takes a leak on the hot wire. You never saw anything so funny in your life when this puke was trying to figure out what the hell was happening to him. He couldn't put it away. He was just jumping up and down waving his tallywhacker all over the place."

"Jesus, guys, we don't have time for this shit! What did you find out about the buildings, T. C.?"

"I can make confetti out of this whole compound, piece of cake. The Dutch built this place for a temporary facility, and that was a hundred years ago."

"Listen, brother, we have to get going. Give Dick a bear hug for me. We'll be in touch with the action plan for Friday."

"I'll give Dick a bear hug for you, but you're not his little brother anymore, you heap much bigger than him now. How tall are you anyway? The last time we saw you, you were tiny little Indian brave who gave everyone fits."

"I'm six-three, so I got you by a couple of inches."

"Well, little brother, I'm taller than Dick and older by two minutes."

Rick and Dick were twins, which was uncommon in our tribe, and they were as close as white on rice. It was a real blow to the tribe when word came they'd been killed in action. I think the shamans knew all along their status, for they knew the future and didn't want to interfere with the natural flow of things.

I told Rick not to say anything to the civilians, because we didn't want anyone to appear nervous or doing anything out of the ordinary.

"Rick, get yourselves and the trio here at the escape tunnel right after chow, and be sure to be here at 1700. The fast movers will be here at 1800, and Champion will set his HE for 1800 as well. Champion will be here the night before to set out his stuff.

"See you brother—have to go."

97

"So long, redskin; please bring back the cavalry and save our asses. Can you imagine an Indian asking for the cavalry? Damn! What are we coming to?"

T. C. and I headed back to the OP after a bit too long at the compound. Heto was about to have a fit and said, "What the hell took you guys so long? I was on the verge of coming to save your clumsy asses."

I explained the situation to him. He calmed down a little and listened as I told him it was like magic, finding my two brothers alive and well. The gods were looking out for the Toms brothers!

"You know, Heto, if Primrose's people hadn't been abducted, we wouldn't have found my brothers, and they could very well have been vaporized when the fast movers got here to level this dump."

"Toms, your shamans must have powerful medicine, and along with my gods, we'll have lots of lightning coming our way."

CHAPTER 16

Vietnam

I called for pickup at 1000 hours at our original LZ just across the border into Vietnam. We covered our tracks and put the OP back in its original condition, making our presence undetectable. With a three-hour hump to be on time, our little team headed out at 0700. It was not what we wanted to do, but we had to leave a fairly visible trail for the trek back into Laos and then a very likely hot pursuit coming out. With all the new guys coming in with us and the POWs and civilians coming out, we would not have time for all the cloak-and-dagger shit.

When we arrived at the landing zone, T. C. Champion took another look around and decided it was not a problem to make a pad the size we needed. The sound of the Huey was the best sound on earth if it was coming to get you, and the First Cav was right on time—they are punctual!

The ride back to home base was uneventful. As I rode along trying to have the courage to fly like an eagle, I was thinking that I was now third in line for tribal chief, but nonetheless chief of this motley crew. When Captain Schroud had put us down on the tarmac, I thanked him for the limo service and told him Primrose would get in touch about time schedules. He lifted off with the usual cloud of red dust and wagged his tail.

Our three-man recon team headed over to the scout sniper platoon area looking for Primrose to fill our leader in on what we found and recommendations for further action. As usual, Primrose was nowhere to be found. He'd have to find us, which would be easy for him, because he had a nose for getting us into trouble. With the blink of his eye, we would be in the shit!

Just as we were dropping our gear, Corporal Martin came walking in with the latest news, telling us our leader Corporal Primrose and about twenty other assholes were in the brig. Martin talks so slow you want to yank the words out of his mouth, which would be easy with my sharp Indian knife.

"Toms, Primrose was over at the EM club and was in the process of getting shit-faced, when he had a few words with some Special Forces guys, and one thing led to another, which included a few blows thrown, which then turned into a full-scale riot. So they all wound up in the brig, but will be released this afternoon, because the SF guys are all due to hit the bush tonight."

"Hey, Martin, you were speaking of the devil—here he comes now."

"I can see, Toms. Wow, look at that fat lip and shiner; somebody must have nailed him good."

Walking up to his motley crew, Primrose announced, "I believe in magic, you guys tell me everything is good to go! In the meantime, don't let the fat lip and colorful eye fool you, the opposition looks sliced and diced.

"After we got locked up, the reason for the altercation kinda got lost and a good time was had by all, except the military police. I found out the SF guys can out drink me two-to-one. I'll have to work on that one and train more. Anyway, fill me in on the big picture!"

I said, "We think the mission is a qualified go, and we can do the job without getting anyone killed. It'll be tricky with the time frame, but nothing we can't overcome. I say, yes, let's go!"

"Okay Toms. And you speak for T. C. and Heto?"

"Hell, yes."

"Okay, let's head over to see the captain—and by the way, how was the trio?"

"She is fine!"

CHAPTER 17

The Mission

The captain was speaking in a rather high-pitched voice, on the verge of ripping my ass a new one!

"Let's get this straight, Corporal Zachary Taylor Primrose."

I hate it when the captain refers to me by rank and full name. It can mean only one thing: no atta-boy shit is coming. I stood at attention as he continued to ream me.

"You intend to take five choppers, three of which are First Cav and two Marine—nice of you to use some of your own—into an unauthorized area, carrying twenty or more people, and drop them off in some of the thickest jungle on the planet. Then they hump through the jungle to a compound that officially doesn't exist and snatch seven people from under the noses of the NVA and VC. Four of the people are POWs, of which two have been declared dead for over six years, and in the process you pick up three civilians who are also supposed to be dead. With all of them in tow, you just walk out of the compound, plant enough HE to level the facility and then hump it back to the LZ, while the compound and tunnels go up like the Fourth of July! Your HE guy is a certified Section 8, who should be in a mental institution, along with the other loose cannons you have chosen for your extraction team. This is going to happen just before a flight of F-4s is supposed to make a parking lot out of the whole area. How am I doing so far, Primrose? Have I got it about right?"

"Yes sir."

"You know, Primrose, between the five of you, your IQs put together would be lower than whale shit."

"Yes sir."

"Primrose, I became a Marine officer to lead men in combat, and on my last tour I did just that, but this time I'm the leader of a group of Marines who would all qualify for that Section 8, with your powder monkey leading the way, and that's before we even talk about that crazy fucking Indian you have on your payroll. But I'm stuck with you. I really don't want to get killed being involved in this crackpot scheme of yours. Every time you open your mouth, I see visions of going home in a body bag, meeting those great chiefs in the sky, and that's not what I had in mind for the future. So, Primrose, let's put all the pieces together and make a realistic mission out of them! It's time to get serious about this harebrained scheme of yours, because it's not a future event anymore, it's game time, the green flag is about to drop! I have questions that need answers. Number one is—how are you going to explain the sudden appearance of three dead musicians, two dead POWs, and two POWs no one has ever heard of? Number two is—how do you plan to keep your asses from being crispy critters when the F-4s come screaming in to kill half the officer corps of the VC and NVA, if something goes wrong on your end? You could get in the way of some very important events and reveal the air strike."

"Sir, we're planning to have the trio head to Thailand and the POWs to division. The trio will say they had an opportunity to escape when they were being moved to a new location near the border with

Thailand. I have made arrangements with a civilian plane to pick them up at a little-used airstrip and then on to Bangkok. You don't want to know any more about the plane or pilot! We drop the POWs off just inside Vietnam, and they hump it to division. They'll show up with a story of getting into the tunnels during the air assault and making their way to freedom. As long as no one gets wind of the mission, we can get away with it. Piece of cake."

"Shit, Primrose, I could have come up with something better than that when I was in the sixth grade, for crying out loud."

"Sir, division may think the civilians and POWs are lying or even know they are, but what can they do? Two problems have been solved for them—three, actually. One, two, three: the civilians show up in Thailand; the POWs come out of the jungle; and the air strike kills half the NVA and VC officer corps. They couldn't bring charges against anyone, or it would come out that they had bombed a compound with the good guys still there and they knew it. All they can do is try and take credit for saving everyone. Division will have a hands-off policy, and as long as we don't get caught in the act, we'll skate. Chances are we'll all be dead anyway, so it won't matter!"

"Primrose, I hope that last statement was a poor attempt at humor?"

"Yes sir, it was."

"Primrose, this whole affair has gaping holes, but all things considered, I like unconventional warfare, and this is right up my alley. Let's get the ball rolling!"

"Sir, I truly believe in my heart of hearts that we can make this mission a success. We have the expertise, the equipment, and most of all the determination to relieve our enemy of their spoils. Our quest is noble, and there is no substitute for freedom. We can make this happen!"

"Primrose, you get with the First Cav and set up a timetable for their choppers, and I'll get with the Marine wing-wipers and secure a couple of their choppers."

As Captain Easy was speaking, I couldn't help but wonder how all this was going to turn out. If a bunch of people were killed and we didn't save anybody, it would be my fault. Shit!

"Primrose, are you listening?"

"Yes sir, was just thinking—nothing important."

As Captain Easy was getting into who was going on the mission, I suggested that we needed Martin for sure. He would be our long-distance insurance.

"Listen up, here is how it we'll play it. Primrose, Champion, Heto, Toms, Martin, and myself will be the core and then four more for ground cover at the LZ and four along the trail to cover our asses going in and coming out. We are getting a little crowded."

When the captain was getting into some of the details, I headed over to meet Captain Schroud on his milk run and told him we had things all squared away for a go on Friday. He said good luck and that he'd be on time, ready to kick some ass. When we departed, he waved and said, "Until then, my friend."

After my visit with Captain Schroud, I headed over to check with Knight. After a little chit-chat, I told him what we were up to. He almost passed out. He said, "That F-4 raid, my friend Primrose, is the most secret operation since Overlord during WWII. How the hell did you find out about it, let alone spread it around to twenty or thirty people? Primrose, are you out of your fucking mind? If division finds out what you're up to, you and your entire team will be dead meat and shot at sunrise, and no one will even blink. Damn, what have you got yourself into? Whatever it is, I want in."

I'd never seen Knight so animated and blown up like a bullfrog, so I told him, "You can't go, Knight, it's all set up and the table is full, besides I need you here to report any changes on this end. We'll be meeting for the last time on Thursday, so if you don't come by or call we can assume everything is good to go. But if anything comes up, and I mean *anything*—let me know."

"Okay, okay. Jesus, I get the message. But I still want in."

"I'll see you when we get back. If things were to go bad, you wouldn't want to be aboard a sinking ship. If you hear anything, it'll be our last face-to-face. Everything from then on will be by radio. May the chiefs in the happy hunting ground send Toms some good juju for the good guys on this one and give us a couple more easy days.'"

"Okay, Primrose, I'll keep you posted."

#

Thursday evening when all were present, the captain called for everyone to report their status, and when all the reports were in, he decided the mission was a go. The captain wished everyone well and was about to dismiss the troops when Knight came rushing in. "I have some news— good or bad, I don't know. Division has moved the air strike up to 1300 hours instead of 1800, because they figure the F-4s need more light to get on target. Let it also be noted that my liberal interpretation of the words *top secret* could have me drawn and quartered. I also request a spot on the team."

"Not this time, Knight, you just proved why you're needed at division. You know a lowly captain like me could never get that kind of information."

We gathered around like a football huddle waiting for the quarterback to lay out the next play, only this time it was Captain Easy speaking. The whistle was about to blow and the game to begin. The whole team was on edge and wanting to get things moving. Nervous energy was like static electricity going through the huddle.

The captain, after digesting the news from Knight, said, "Toms, Champion, and Heto, you'll go in five hours earlier tonight. Toms, you get with your brothers, give them a heads-up, and tell them to bring the civilians in on the escape. I'll arrange for an early chopper ride for you three, and Primrose, you get with Schroud and see if our recent news will upset anything on his end."

"Yes sir."

I was listening to the captain, again thinking I was responsible for the whole chain of events, and it could be roses or body bags. Damn!

"Listen up. For the rest of us zero hour is 0700 Friday. Be on the tarmac and ready to mount out. Champion, did you get everything you needed from supply?"

"Yes sir. It's all packed and ready for action. We can jump off anytime you say, sir."

Toms and Heto chimed in with an *aye, aye sir.*

"Primrose, did T. W. Dons ask anything in return for his help?"

"No sir, he just asked to go along, but I said no, we're full up. What he has done for us is way beyond the call of duty, with lots of HE, weapons, night vision, radios, ammo, etc., and a couple of Hawk missiles if we want. He's a real dealer, a dog-robber first class."

#

The captain had a chopper for our three night fighters, and off they went to get the ball rolling. The rest of the team headed back to the scout sniper area to prepare for the mission. D-Day was within hours, and it would bring the choppers to give us a short ride and deposit us into the thick jungle for my well-intended mission. Choke time was over, it was pucker time; the green flag had dropped.

I called Schroud on a landline. "Captain, the fast movers have been pushed up five hours. We're looking at 1300 hours now."

"No problem, Zach, I can fix my end; actually, we're ready now if you needed it. Working for a general has its up side, but if you fuck up and make him look bad, it's a very steep slide down. Right now, Zach, my sway with the general is way up and we're good to go."

Nice to have such confidence on our team. Like T. W. Dons over in supply, he gets the job done, with no problem too big or small. In civilian life the two dog-robbers would be in the slammer, so it's a good thing this war came along and gave them the opportunity of a lifetime.

I for one hoped Friday wouldn't be our last time to see the sunrise. Some say it's better to be lucky than good, which may or may not be a good saying, but we were very good at what we did and with a little help from the shamans, as Toms said was coming, only we couldn't see it, maybe the good guys would win this one.

CHAPTER 18

Laos

The LZ was just as we left it, so the chopper dropped me the great Indian warrior, Champion, and Heto right in the same tracks as before. How do these mix masters set down in the exact same spot? The chopper lifted off and wagged his tail as he disappeared into the night.

Champion began to set out his HE right away, and with a little help from his warrior buds, the LZ was soon ready to become a king-size area, big enough for four choppers if needed, because we had a good chance of fighting our way back here. Hopefully we wouldn't have any dead or wounded to encumber our flight. Preparation of the site was critical for a quick, smooth exit—or a good place to feel the reality that Custer must have felt.

I told Heto to lead the way back to the OP, with Champion in the middle and me the great Indian fighter bringing up our six.

The return trip was as routine as you could get in this world of hanging vines, tall grass, and tree limbs. Heto stopped short of the OP, just to make sure we hadn't been discovered. I still couldn't believe these stupid fuckers hadn't sent out small roving patrols around the fence area. Good for us and tough shit for them. It was pucker time, so I told Heto to stay at the OP and cover our ass.

He retorted, "Good thing to leave me here at OP, I'm the best and you two could screw up a free bingo game. Now get going before I decide not to be good sport and cover your ass."

Champion and I headed down the tunnel, for our next move was to get with my brothers and begin setting the charges.

When we got to the ladder, it hadn't been disturbed, which was really good news. The dumb shits never even ran a check on their escape routes, so score another one for the good guys.

After Champion got the cover off, I started my Indian birdcalls, to get Rick and Dick's attention. Just as I was about to send my second round of calls, I heard my brother Dick whisper in my ear, "Not so loud, man, you want the gooks to hear you?"

"Jesus, Dick, you scared the shit out of me. You guys need to stop this creeping-up-on-me stuff."

"Relax, Tom, we knew you were here. The shamans keep us informed at all times through visions."

"Well, you sure have a sense of humor after being a POW for six or seven years."

"Thanks, but we owe it all to the shamans, who have let us know the outcome of this party, and we've known for some time."

At about the time I was getting over the scare Dick had given me, Rick came sneaking up and did another number on me and said, "You need to be more like Dick and me, little brother, and get back in touch with your spirit side, because you have lost your Indian ways of being able to sense your surroundings. We'll get you tuned up."

"Look guys, this is serious shit, quit the fooling around. Dick, take Champion around to set his HE."

"Okay, brother, but you need to lighten up a little. The chiefs are watching over us, no sweat on the outcome."

"Yes sir, Dick, I'll try and be a little more in tune with the spirits, but for now, Rick and I will head over to the trio's building. We need to bring them in on this mission."

Before we reached the trio's building, Rick, with a big smile, said, "Now it's time to be good Indians, clever and quiet. The gooks may not be watching the outside, but they watch the inside very closely, so we have to be sneaky Indians tonight."

We walked, ran, and crawled over to the trio's building, and then Rick used a knocking code they had devised to communicate. Someone inside responded, and we were admitted without being seen by the guards.

Fred, Jack, and Rhonda were really happy to see us and listened intently to the plan for the following day. Rhonda was pleased to learn Zach had worked so hard to get the rescue operational. They were also pissed to learn that the trio were to have been sacrificed in the name of the war effort and doubled pissed that division knew they were at the camp and never mounted a rescue attempt.

Fred and Jack thought they should have been treated better after getting through WWII, and Rhonda being a civilian should have been a priority package for a rescue attempt. They all agreed to do their part; after all they were actors, and their role was a piece of cake.

Sneaking around the compound was a given for my two Indian brothers. The two had been doing it for a long time in this compound and others like it.

After the buildings were loaded with HE, Dick and Champion returned to the tunnels and loaded them as well, leaving the escape tunnel for last. With that done, I got everyone together in the escape tunnel to go over the plan once more. The civilians were ready and willing to do their part, no questions asked. I had Champion set the buildings for 1255 and the tunnels for 1300, except for the escape tunnel, which we would blow in sections if there was hot pursuit.

It would be one hell of a show if there was anyone left to watch it—the fuckers wouldn't know what hit them! The buildings, tunnels, and the air assault—boom, boom, and boom again. With the shamans on our side, we couldn't lose.

With our work done for the night, Champion and I headed back down the tunnel to the OP, hoping Heto didn't try to shoot us. Heto was going to be really pissed because we took so long, but we were glad the Okinawan was on our team; he was the best there was in the jungle.

While we were running down the tunnel Champion was rubbing his hands together and grinning from ear to ear, saying he couldn't wait to pull the pin Friday. I think Champion is real close to being a little around the bend, when it comes to using any kind of explosives. Champion said his whole family was crazy about blowing things up, that it was an inherited trait. He found it exciting even if he could only hear the explosion and feel the rumble and not see the fire and brimstone.

When we got back to the OP, Heto made us give the password, *Kemosabe,* to harass us, because he knew damn well who we were, but he was into the cowboy and Indian movie shit. Working with a real Indian was a thrill for him; with a smile he gave the counter, *hi-ho Silver.* Heto was wearing Indian-made moccasins from Japan—fitting for the chief scout on this mission.

We settled in to wait for the dawn to show its beautiful light rays through the thick emerald foliage. What was left of our short night was disappearing rapidly.

CHAPTER 19

On the Tarmac, Vietnam

Standing on the runway as our taxi service hovered, about to touch down, was easy as the adrenalin was pumping, getting the body ready for the mission. It was time for us to head into the mouth of the lion; my thoughts were of Rhonda and how many things could go wrong and how many had to go right to have a successful mission. My mind was going a fast as the bullet train in Japan with imaginings of the pitfalls ahead. During the boarding process, it was quiet as a church, with each team member into his own thoughts about the coming events and each hoping for the same ending: mission accomplished without any WIAs or KIAs. But each man knew that there was hardly ever a mission without casualties. Murphy's law says someone will get hit.

The captain was in full combat mode, along with the rest of us, and it was interesting to note how each man gets ready within himself for the rigors of combat. Some say nothing, other laugh or talk non-stop, while other just stare out the hatch, but all are ready to do their part when the mission unfolds.

Our limo service lifted off right on time, heading for the border with Laos. The captain had a grin from ear to ear. He was finally in his element—leading Marines into combat. The true test of a leader is to lead his troops into the valley of death and come out intact as a unit and to the man, with mission accomplished.

The flight was short, and as we came over the LZ, it was just as Toms had described it. It needed Champion to pull the trigger later and make it look like a Sears and Roebuck parking lot in Los Angeles. Because of the skilled pilots going in, we only had a three-foot drop to the ground, which was a whole lot better than a ten-foot rope-skill test.

#

Captain Easy positioned four troops around the landing zone for our cover coming out. He told them to look over the site and watch out for the HE Champion had set. He told the troopers that Champion would be the first one back to alert them and blow the LZ. Martin would also stay back to be our long-distance cover and would pick off anyone getting too close in their pursuit.

With everyone safely on the deck, we headed into the jungle, following the well-marked trail left by the others. The hump was easy, and the captain left four troops along the trail for additional cover for the return trip.

When we arrived at the OP, Toms was there to greet us. Heto and Champion had already headed down the tunnel.

"Toms! "

"Yes sir."

"How do we look?"

"Good to go, sir."

"That's good news. Along with the textbook drop at the LZ, things are going rather well."

"You know, Captain, I was getting worried about all you white eyes getting lost without trusted Indian scout. I was beginning to think Heto and I would have to pull this mission by ourselves."

After all the good-natured humor, which covered everyone's raw nerves, we headed down the tunnel with Toms in the lead, followed by me and then the captain. There was precious little time to waste; all hell was going to break loose very soon. We wanted to be as far from the camp as possible when it went up and the air strike came in.

The trek down the tunnel was a piece of cake all the way to the ladder. Heto and Champion were waiting at the base of the ladder. When we were all gathered together, the captain told Heto to open the hatch. Heto climbed up and pulled the cover aside, and standing there were the Indian brothers holding a tarp over the area of the hole. The two brothers were grinning like a couple of Cheshire cats. They must have been having a vision about then. In just seconds, the trio came sliding down the ladder, knocking Heto to the deck. Fred, Jack, and Rhonda came down one, two, three. How could a woman look so good under such horrid conditions?

The hardest part of the mission so far was getting me and Rhonda apart.

The captain said, "We don't have time for the happy reunion shit, Primrose, there'll be a more appropriate time for you to greet each other properly. I will shoot you if you don't break it up!"

Reluctantly we let go, and I headed the trio down the tunnel to the OP and freedom's door. Captain Easy got the POWs down, closed the hatch for the last time, and headed them towards the OP.

With the buildings already rigged for destruction, the tunnel was the last thing to be rigged. Champion and Heto began to finish that job as they followed the rest of the crew down the tunnel, setting it up as they went for its ultimate implosion.

As everyone was running down the tunnel, all ears were listening for the telltale sounds of pounding feet, escape sirens, or—worse yet—the sound of automatic weapons.

I led the rescue team with our charges down the tunnel to the OP in record time, stopping to check for pursuit from the tunnel or from above. The captain counted heads and we didn't see or hear anything, which brought to mind thoughts that we might actually get away with this harebrained scheme.

There was no unusual activity from any direction. It was hard to believe these fuckers thought the jungle was all they needed to cover their asses. Score one more for the good guys!

Just behind us came Champion and Heto, finishing up with the HE along the tunnel deck.

Champion was like a new father the way he handled the explosives. Passing along the words "fire in the hole," he set the timer, and we headed into the jungle and freedom.

The captain sent Heto and Toms to the point, with the civilians and the POWs at midships with him and the radio operator. Champion and I would bring up our six and take on any bad guys who might have gotten wind of our escape.

The trek was going as planned with no major delays. After a couple of hours the captain got on the radio and called "Abracadabra," our LZ team, to let them know we were on schedule. Their reply was no activity on their end, and the "Magic Man" had called—he was inbound and on time!

This was all going too easy. The hair was starting to get stiff on my neck, which meant Murphy was about to show his ugly head again.

Something was bound to fuck things up. When we took a break I asked the Indians if they had any feelings from the shamans. Their reply was negative, but their hair was also standing on end. I wondered how that was possible, since they didn't have much hair. But the feeling was mutual—something was in the air, and it was bad juju.

When the captain declared the break over, Champion moved out to the point so he would be the first to the LZ and begin his task of making it a suitable landing spot for the incoming choppers.

As the column marched along, the security we had left behind fell in and joined us for the short distance to the LZ. When we had gotten within a mile of the LZ, we met Champion and our LZ team heading back towards us to clear the area for the HE to go. The captain halted the column, and we spread out on either side of the trail.

Champion waved his arms and using his fingers started counting down from ten; when his last finger disappeared, we heard and felt the compound explode. Jesus, what an explosion, with a shock wave that almost knocked us down. Champion was grinning like a kid who just tossed a cherry bomb into the high school gym. The tunnels imploded next and his grin got even bigger.

About the time the smoke was blowing away from the compound, the F-4s came screaming over our heads, so low the tops of the jungle trees were singed and wilted. What a surprise they were in for, not having any problem finding their targets. What came next was another series of ground-shaking explosions and shock waves hitting us big time. Champion was still grinning with a crazed look in his eyes, enjoying every moment. As the sound of the destruction reached us, the LZ went up, and we were caught in the middle of rumblings going both directions.

Just as we emerged from the jungle canopy, the radio started screaming at us, with the radio operator getting it simultaneously from Magic Man and Abracadabra. Both had a high-pitched excited sound to their voices.

Captain Easy answered Magic Man first. "Magic Man, this is Hocus-Pocus."

"Hocus-Pocus, I have some bad news and some good news, which do you want first?"

"Just spit it out, Magic Man, we don't have time to be dicking around!"

"Well, Captain Easy, the bad news is there is a battalion-size NVA force on your left flank, now shooting the hell out of your LZ. The good news is we're here to cover your withdrawal, and it will be a pleasure to keep them busy."

"Hocus-Pocus, this is Abracadabra, the LZ is ready and the choppers are on the way in, the red smoke is up and we're in one hell of a firefight. It's one hot-ass LZ, and you need to get your butts up here pronto, sir."

"Ten-four Abracadabra, we're in sight." We hustled up to the LZ as fast as we could. When we arrived, we could see the firefight had been grossly understated—there was a full-fledged battle going on.

#

With our additional firepower and the sharpshooting of Martin, whose bolt action was giving a near automatic sound, and the First Cav boring in on them, the enemy had to back off a little. This encouraged the First Cav to come in with a vengeance and suppress them even further. With this opening, our Marine choppers came in and we scrambled aboard quickly and lifted off without too much fire hitting its target. In our haste, we left Martin and had to make a quick return, snatching up Martin between bursts of machine-gun fire.

Martin was grinning from eat to ear, just like Champion, and yelled over the noise of the battle and the sound of the Huey, "Never had so much fun in my life. If you love to shoot the bad gays, this is like being in a whorehouse in Nevada, with unlimited credit!" Then, spotting Rhonda sitting next to me, he got a little red faced and said, "Sorry Rhonda, didn't see you sitting there."

"That's okay Martin, I'll personally get you a credit card for helping free us from that cesspool back there."

As I watched the two yelling back and forth I thought, There's a major battle going on around us, and their thoughts are about apologies and credit cards! Jesus!

CHAPTER 20

Marine Recon Outpost

"Little Dog, this is Big Dog, come in Little Dog."

"Hello Big Dog, this is Little Dog."

"Little Dog, what's your twenty?"

The radio operator pushed the handset to Sergeant Williams. "It's Recon HQ, they want to know our position."

Sergeant Williams took the handset, wondering what the hell was going on, and said, "Sergeant Williams here, we're at the point discussed at the briefing, which is on the small hill just across the border from Laos, above the old smuggler's trail, which you guys said was not in use."

"Yes, you're right, Sergeant Williams, it hasn't been used in years. It was first used by thieves, then the French, and now who knows. It's your job to watch the trail and make sure who is or isn't using it these days."

"Big Dog, we read you loud and clear, but do you suppose your information on the trail might be a little dated? We are looking at an NVA battalion coming down the trail as we speak, and if they make us, our odds for survival are near zero. Three recon Marines and two snipers may be a force to reckon with, but in this situation discretion may be the better part of valor—request permission to disappear!"

"Little Dog, negative, keep you position and report all movement. You're supposed to be invisible. Remember your training."

"Big Dog, we read you and request air cover and arty, in case of emergency. Big Dog, we've just heard some very large explosions coming from inside Laos! The NVA guys heard it and have stopped dead in their tracks. There went another boomer and another. Jesus, what the hell's going on? It's rock and roll time again, this time just inside the border, where someone just blew a perfect circle in the open. It looks just like a large cookie cutter was used to clear the area. Big Dog, a flight of F-4s just flew over us going into Laos, and they were low enough to read the numbers on their helmets. I say again—what the hell is going on?"

"Little Dog, sit tight and report, you are the eyes and ears of the battalion. The F-4s were expected, but not the other thing going on."

"Big Dog, we're hearing transmissions like Hocus-Pocus, Abracadabra, and Magic Man. We also see three First Cav choppers. Two are gunships and one is on high, who seems to be directing traffic. Behind the First Cav are three Marine helos—looks like a parade is forming up!"

"Little Dog, what have you pinheads been smoking? There are no joint Army-Marine operations going in that area or any other."

"Big Dog, listen, the NVA have just opened up on the cookie-cutter landing zone, and they're getting lots of return fire. Please listen to the radio traffic!"

"Hocus-Pocus, this is Magic Man, we'll engage the NVA battalion, we see they have already fired on the LZ. Abracadabra, we'll take some of the heat off you and keep the door open."

"Marine air, this is Hocus-Pocus, continue your pickup at the LZ."

"Big Dog, this is Little Dog, the First Cav has engaged the enemy battalion and caught them in the open. Jesus, they are ripping them to shreds. What a sight! Two tours, and I've never seen anything like it."

"Little Dog, I say again, there are no Army-Marine joint operations in that area. There was only an air strike scheduled for today, and that was top secret, known by only a very few."

"Big Dog, this is Little Dog. There are now twenty or so people running out of the jungle for the LZ, and they aren't all military. There are civilians in the group and some guys who appear to be POWs. Jesus, now I've seen everything—there is a big blonde woman with the group. The rest are Marines and one oriental-looking guy, plus a few Marines around the LZ, and they are real busy right now. We also see a Marine scout sniper in a large tree having a field day—he'll run out of ammo before he runs out of targets. Our position here is like being on the fifty-yard line at a football game."

"Little Dog, get the numbers off the choppers."

"Big Dog, the choppers have no numbers, just First Cav and USMC is visible. My team is getting a real live combat lesson up close and personal. We request permission to engage!"

"Little Dog, permission denied, just keep reporting."

"Big Dog, the First Cav is doing a number on the NVA regulars and the three Marine air are coming down to the LZ to pick up their cargo."

"Little Dog, we want numbers from the choppers."

"Big Dog, I say again, there are no numbers, and the Marine air has picked up their cargo and are on their way south. Whoops, one is coming back—they overlooked the sniper and are returning for him. The First Cav guys have disengaged and are heading south, they must have run out of ammo. Guess the show is over."

"Big Dog, did you hear that last transmission?"

"Ten-four Little Dog."

"Big Dog, whoever these guys were, they just had a turkey shoot, the NVA may as well have been in a barrel. They kicked some big-time ass today, and whoever put this show on the road had a lot better intelligence than we do. Not only did they kick butt, they probably saved our ass in the process. Our thanks to somebody."

"Little Dog, you have a sniper team with you, is that correct?"

"Ten-four, Big Dog."

"Little Dog, stand by."

"Little Dog, this is Colonel Washington. Sergeant Williams, do you remember me?"

"Yes sir."

"Sergeant Williams, this what I want you to do. When the NVA think the air cover is gone for good, they'll come out to check for wounded and drag their dead back into the jungle. Have the snipers whack a few of them to keep them busy, while you take the rest of your people down to the battle scene and get me a live prisoner. I would prefer an officer. Search the dead for useful information, etc. You know the drill."

"Sir, I read you loud and clear, but my sniper team is green, it's their first time in the bush. They'll be shooting around us as we search. Not a happy thought, sir."

"Sergeant Williams, they are well-trained Marines, right? So go get my prisoner, and a body count while you're at it. I need to find out where this large of a force came from and what unit they belong to and how they got there."

"Yes sir, we're on our way."

"Keep the channel open, Sergeant."

"Yes sir."

CHAPTER 21

Division

"Colonel Washington, this is General Tumwater, from Division HQ."

"Yes sir, how may I help you, General?"

"Something very big happened in your area today, Colonel! As I understand it, you're not aware of all the events, is that correct?"

"Yes sir."

"That something happened just before, during, or after a top secret bombing run! According to the flyboys, their target was a compound, and it was a smoldering mass of sticks when they arrived. They dumped their ordinance anyway just to be sure the target was completely destroyed. No one could have survived the first assault, let alone the second. I want to know who, what, and where, Colonel! Somebody was at the compound before our fast movers. I want to know who they were and where they came from."

"Sir, I've checked with every company and battalion within range, Army and Marine. They all replied their personnel and equipment were present and/or accounted for. The First Cav was the most negative, saying that if their guys wiped out an NVA battalion, who would care how or when, just congratulate them and give them some medals and a little R & R in Aussie land. They wouldn't exchange any information with us. As far as the civilians go, we are in the dark with them as well, and the POWs are another mystery—we've not heard of any in this area."

"Here's the question, Colonel: how did six choppers and a large number of military personnel with lots of firepower show up in the exact area and time as a secret bombing run? How could this happen without the knowledge of anyone in the whole of the Far East? I want answers, Colonel, and you're the guy who's going to get them for me! You know whose ass is in the ringer right now!"

"Yes sir, consider your orders done sir, I'll be all over it!"

"Colonel, you know shit runs downhill, and you're standing in the path. Good day, Colonel."

"Damn! What did I do to deserve this?"

CHAPTER 22

Dispersing

The Marine choppers dropped the POWs off with a two-day hump to division, where their story might or might not be believed, but it didn't matter, because they'd be welcomed back, and given medals and parades for surviving and escaping. The only thing division can do is try and take credit somehow for the results.

We won't care, for we accomplished the impossible, and we'll just smile and be happy that we all came through the ordeal without a scratch.

The Marine chopper with the trio aboard landed at a small abandoned airstrip, where a private plane chartered in advance was on the runway and ready for takeoff. I was given permission to go along as security, for obvious reasons. All the other Marines and First Cav headed back to their respective units, with the satisfaction of a job well done.

Captain Schroud called Captain Easy to thank him for inviting them along on such a rewarding mission and said, "Captain Easy, that mission was a great experience, and we had a damn good time, with the NVA battalion being the icing on the cake. Getting those POWs and civilians was a major high for us. From the intel going around, the enemy had planned a major offensive, but now don't have enough officers to staff a Boy Scout troop. It was a pleasure to piss off the brass in all of I-Corps, and that alone was worth the risk. Best of all, they don't know who pulled off such a daring raid and won't ever find out the truth—what more could a guy ask for?"

Everyone made it back to their areas without mishap, from a job well done. No medals, no slaps on the back, just personal satisfaction that they had given the enemy a very hard slap from which it would not soon recover.

CHAPTER 23

Thailand

After landing in Thailand, we took a taxi directly to the Oriental Hotel in Bangkok, one of the finest hotels in the Far East. We booked three rooms and agreed to meet first thing in the morning for breakfast. Jack sent out for a tailor to have new clothes made for the trio, since they'd lost everything in their travels. Rhonda and I disappeared. It would have been so easy to just keep going and fly home, but we had obligations to the Corps, and her tour wasn't finished.

The first evening with Rhonda was like a first date, only with no limits. The room service guy made umpteen trips to the room, with everything from steak to ice cream. The hotel surely almost ran out of hot water and towels. The evening went all too fast. The daylight through the open window brought us back to reality, and we headed to Fred's room for breakfast. Rhonda had only a hotel robe for clothes, but the tailor promised more by noon.

At Fred's room we had steak and eggs, hot coffee, real orange juice, and toast. The smell of real coffee and orange juice was overwhelming. What do they say? Absence makes the heart grow fonder. For sure in my case with Rhonda—smelling her perfume once again was overpowering.

I asked Rhonda, "So how were you treated by the NVA and VC?"

"Zach, as long as the band kept playing, they treated us rather well, but when we didn't play and they began to tire of us, it was scary. They enjoyed looking at the big American blonde, and that made me want to gag. The compound was half R & R and half strategy meetings and the like. Big Commie planning sessions and indoctrination. Those dumb shits even tried to sway us with their red bullshit—what a joke that was. The officers weren't bad, they kept their hands to themselves and treated us with a little more respect than the others. We played mostly at night, and it was like a jam session for us."

"Jack, when did you and Fred figure something was up, or did you not know anything until the Indian brothers pulled you in on the escape plan?"

"Zach, it was the other day that we noticed the Indians acting a little different—not so much that the moron guards would notice, just little things. They were a little too happy with their work, acting a little like the cat that just ate the mouse. It was such a relief when they told us of the plan and who was behind the whole affair. Rhonda was right, she knew you were out there somewhere trying to find us and mount a rescue. But why did we come back to Bangkok, instead of Da Nang, Zach?"

"It goes something like this, Fred. We couldn't compromise the bombing mission by division, because division didn't know what we were up to. If they ever find out who was involved in this rescue, it would be dungeons for us, maybe even execution. We stepped on a lot of toes getting this operation together, as we appropriated a lot of government property without permission, and the number of military and government regulations we sidestepped would choke a

Philadelphia lawyer. Hopefully the brass will never find out the truth. And after you guys and the POWs show up, they'll be hard pressed to shoot anyone for doing what they should have done, before we did it. Division knows something extraordinary happened, but doesn't know what or how or by whom. We didn't screw up their bombing raid, we just got there first. The brass has only one way to go: try and take credit for the rescue and helping the POWs. We have been very lucky during this whole affair, and we've had some very capable and dedicated men risk their lives for us and do so with a smile."

I left Bangkok after two wonderful days with Rhonda in the Flower of the Far East. I had loved every minute of it. We never left the room and wore out the room service waiter, eating everything on the menu. Rhonda was certainly an expensive date. But those two days made the whole journey worthwhile.

The trio headed for the American Embassy to tell a tale of escape and how they used some disgruntled VC who wanted to defect as their opening for freedom. Their story ran in the headlines all over the world, and about the same time the POWs showed up out of the jungle as another miracle took place.

Well, it was the Hocus-Pocus, Abracadabra, and Magic Man show that pulled this rescue off, maybe with a little help from God and the shamans. The chiefs in the sky were on our side on this one—the good guys win one for a change!

Division will investigate, but not with any real intentions of finding anything. The captain is planning a beach party to celebrate our good fortune, and the trio has been invited to be the party's entertainment.

#

Life goes on for us. We have our tours to complete, and I have been assigned to the Scout Sniper Platoon for the rest of my tour, which I had wanted from the beginning. One lousy typing test sure triggered a huge chain of events.

Toms agreed to be my scout, spotter, and teammate, and suggested as long as he's with me I won't get lost or dead. He didn't want to escort any bodies back home and decided it was his responsibility to keep me away from the grim reaper. I agreed on the condition that he wouldn't do the fingers and ears thing. Toms complained, but agreed to only leave an occasional calling card as a reminder of his presence.

The Toms brothers and the other POWs were treated as heroes as they were flown back to the real world, all neat and clean, with their pockets full of seven years' back pay. The trio continued their tour, heading for Hong Kong and points west.

#

"Primrose, Toms! Captain Easy wants to see you, like yesterday!"

Captain Easy's orderly was a sour puss, with no sense of humor. We knocked on the captain's hatch and requested permission to enter.

"Get your sorry asses in here and stand at attention until further notice!" With his point made, he ordered, "As you were, gentlemen. I have something for you two to consider. It may be illegal, and out of bounds to all military standards, and it's certainly out of the ordinary. You two know about that kind of shit—right?"

"Yes sir, we do."

"Are you interested in a little out-of-bounds duty?"

"Yes sir, we are."

"One man with courage makes a majority."

Andrew Jackson

Thank you: ANNE GEIBERGER

ABOUT THE AUTHOR:

R. Michael Haigwood is a Marine Veteran, life member and past Commandant of the Black Mountain Detachment, Marine Corps League, and a member of the Black Mountain Harley Davidson Owners Group (HOG), He has been a big hole driller, underground diamond driller, heavy equipment operator, hotel bartender, bell hop, black jack dealer, union negotiator, and Senior Olympics athlete. He has been happily married for forty-three years to his high school sweetheart Ronni Sullivan, a retired musician, singer, comedian, and mother who entertained the troops in the Far East, including Vietnam.

LaVergne, TN USA
13 October 2010

200552LV00002B/20/P

9 781438 923048